G000122788

THE POWER
OF THE
Story

TOUCHING THE LIVES OF LISTENERS

ROB HARLEY

■ ────────────────────────────

Published by End Results Publishing Ltd
P O Box 99 433, Newmarket, Auckland
New Zealand

ISBN 0-473-08071-0

© 2001 Rob Harley
All rights reserved
Printed in New Zealand

Typeset and Cover Design by Megan Singleton, Auckland, New Zealand
Printed by Wentforth Print, Auckland, New Zealand

Unless noted otherwise, Scriptures are from the Holy Bible, New International Version. Copyright © 1973, 1978, 1984 by International Bible Society. Used by permission of Zondervan Publishing House. All rights reserved.

For Ali, Ben and Kate

Contents

Acknowledgements

When your journalistic career has been mostly about television, the discipline of painting pictures with words on their own is not easy!

So I want to thank several people for making this all possible. First, Graeme Paris, tireless head of the Willow Creek Associations of both the United Kingdom and New Zealand. He provoked me to write the book and he never let up.

Thanks to Willow Creek Community Church in Chicago for graciously allowing me to reproduce some of the fine teaching that emanates from that astonishing place.

My appreciation also to Phil Guyan of the Christian Broadcasting Association of New Zealand, for his vision of the "Scrubcutter" series, which first got me writing down my stories in an organised way.

Introduction

Great verbal communication is one of the most powerful things in the world. The human voice has the ability to summon whole nations to war, to inspire people to live better and more honorable lives, to take up great causes and change the entire trajectory of where they're going.

Some of the best communication is accomplished with the skilful use of illustrations and stories. Everyone loves stories. We're raised on their entrancing power from the time we are old enough to assemble thoughts and create our own memories. As we grow older, we never lose our interest in stories: Hollywood and ten million authors and journalists know that to be true.

I've written this book because of my own love of story telling. As a journalist and public speaker, I know the raw power of the "for instance". When a writer or speaker moves away from generalisations into the realm of the specific, there is an inevitable surge in **Never make a point without telling a story, and never tell a story without making a point.** interest and often, in understanding. Tests done on audiences show that blood pressure actually rises in a listener when a speaker gets specific!

A pastor friend of mine passed on a most useful observation. He tells budding preachers: "Never make a point without telling a story, and never tell a story without making a point." It's great advice, and springs from the methodology of the greatest teacher of all time – Jesus.

It records in Matthew's gospel that he "used stories to tell all these things to the people." [NCV]. Given that Jesus had just three years to bring about the most complete transformation of human hearts ever attempted, I am amazed he spent so much time telling stories. It's quite clear to me that this is part of what made people marvel at Jesus' teaching, and it's also partly why they felt they were getting something more profound from Him than they'd ever received in the dry and legalistic lessons from the Pharisees.

Jesus knew very well that there's so much power in stories – so much that's memorable. Stories can move us and help us find points of personal identification with timeless truths.

Much of what follows comes from my own experiences as a journalist and a communicator in the spoken word. But the rest of it comes from my years as a pastor and teacher. Those years in ministry taught me that there's nothing like the Word of God; no wisdom, no acquired experience, no knowledge, no philosophy. The Bible is the gentle whisper of the most dynamic friend, father, lover and counselor you could imagine.

I've sat with presidents and world leaders, interviewed the great minds of this planet, covered stories and events that boggle the mind. But after all that, I have concluded that nothing has the power to reach into the soul and shape a life, like God's truths taught by a creative and passionate communicator.

I know what you're about to read will encourage you to be a more effective storyteller and story-finder. I know you will also start approaching your world with two sets of eyes and ears – one set, to marvel and enjoy God's handiwork, while your other eyes and ears gather stories!

Just one note, before we embark: because I've been collecting stories over more than twenty years, the source of some of the tales I have amassed, is a bit uncertain. I have done my best to try to track down and acknowledge authorship of the stories I have included, but I have not been successful in every case.

I trust you'll understand!

Rob Harley
November 2001

–1–

Capturing the Imagination

"Few things are harder to put up with than a good example."
–Mark Twain

"Were not our hearts burning within us while he talked?"
–Luke 24:32

I t was one particular story that first did it for me. I was on an aircraft, coming back from a business trip. Sliding the tape into my walkman at about 26,000 feet somewhere over New Zealand, I had decided to take in the last twenty minutes of a preacher's message before we landed in Auckland. The preacher hit me squarely between my earlobes, with his tale from the Second World War.

I realised years later that maybe I hadn't recalled all the details with pinpoint accuracy, but I'd remembered enough to know the impression made on me by this story.

Each crewmember clenched his teeth and tensed himself, awaiting what seemed the inevitable.

The story was about an American bomber. One night, having dropped its deadly load on a German industrial complex, the bomber, with its crew of young men, turned for home – an airbase in the English countryside. As the B-17 droned through Europe's black night, two things happened almost at once. The probing fingers of Nazi searchlights reached into the sky ahead of the plane, and then, powerful anti-aircraft batteries opened up, sending a barrage of shells towards the homebound squadron.

Like mini-meteors the shells were exploding ahead of the bomber. The crew felt the familiar, sickening apprehension spread through the plane like a clammy mist. The "kill rate" on nights like this often saw less than half the squadron return home. There was no way of avoiding the barrage

– it was too intense and widespread. Each crewmember clenched his teeth and tensed himself, awaiting what seemed the inevitable.

The Miracle Unfolds

Suddenly the first thud rocked the plane – a shell from the guns below had hit the fuselage. Quick prayers, a bracing for the explosion. Then, more thuds, in the wings and the body of the bomber, but at the same time, within seconds, an awesome realisation. The thuds kept coming, the plane trembling with each impact, but as yet, no explosions. After what seemed an eternity, the bomber cleared the field of fire – each man's eyes bulging, mouth hanging open – a mixture of expectation and mad delight. It seemed they'd been badly hit – several times – but they were still flying.

The note said simply "This is all we can do for you now."

The bomber, with gaping holes torn in many places, made it back to its English base. Mechanics and support staff swarmed all over the aircraft as the crew babbled their tale of seeming miraculous deliverance. Within moments, an engineer emerged from under the belly of the plane with an unexploded shell he'd prized free from the gas tanks.

It turned out to be one of about a dozen. The shells were carefully dismantled, and amazingly, contained no explosive charge. All empty, except for one in which they found a carefully scrolled piece of paper. It was written hastily, in pencil, in the Czech language. The note said simply "This is all we can do for you now."

What dawned on the American airmen that morning was awesome. Somewhere in a Nazi munitions factory, Czech slave labourers, who knew full well the awful penalties for sabotage, had taken a huge risk. In an effort to help the Allies win the war, they had made non-exploding shells and had then had the breathtaking courage to let someone know how the redemption of one American bomber crew had been accomplished. [1]

For probably the first time, I understood the power of a great story, the potential impact of a modern-day parable.

Struck By Stories

The story blew my mind. The teacher on the tape used it to make a significant point about courage, and what standing up for the truth sometimes costs. For probably the first time, I understood the power of a great story, the potential impact of a modern-day parable. I saw how easy it would be, using this kind of story, to put real skin on a principle like "Greater love has no man than this, that he lay down his life for his friends." I can't remember anything else about that tape, apart from the story and its application.

It got me thinking: as I cast my mind back over literally thousands of messages I must have heard in my life – the stuff I could readily call to mind from all the teaching I had sat under, was actually pretty limited.

And then it came to me. The things that had made the deepest impressions were stories and the illustrations that preachers had used, to bring colour, life and application to their talks.

"Total Recall" – A Total Myth

The sad truth is that we forget much of what we hear pretty quickly. One survey found that people who'd heard a talk were unable to recall 90 percent of the message three days later, even when given strong reminders. This can be really depressing news for a communicator!

People who'd heard a talk were unable to recall 90 percent of the message three days later.

So how do we enhance people's ability to recall and retain what we say? Probably in several ways, some of which we'll discuss as we go along. For starters, it seems to me, from years of making TV documentaries and listening to talks, that the more "general" a speaker's or broadcaster's remarks, the less likely the hearers are to remember the thrust of the message.

This is where you reach for the power of what I call the "for instance".

It's when you stop looking at the scene with a wide-angle lens and focus in on a real person or situation that the listener or viewer can identify with.

In pursuit of the "for instance," I find myself continually shouting at TV sets and [mentally] shouting at speakers: "Examples! Examples! Give me an example!" Drives people mad if they're trying to watch TV programmes with me, but I can't help myself.

Perhaps the principle is best illustrated by listening every now and then, to our own children. Listening to what my kids say when they come home from school, it's quite clear that the teachers who have used the power of illustration well, have made the most lasting impression.

Getting Martha From the Kitchen

Among some of my colleagues in television current affairs, there's an old catch-cry we sometimes use to describe the ideal story. We call it a "Hey Martha" event. It goes like this: out there in TV Land there is a heck of a lot of apathy and jaded "viewing palates."

Somewhere among those hundreds of thousands of viewers, is a theoretical couple called Harry and Martha. Harry is a bit of a slob. He sits collapsed in front of the TV in a threadbare armchair most nights with a beer in one hand, and a remote control in the other, and grumbles continually that "there's nothin' on worth watchin'." Martha spends most of her time in other rooms of the house doing stuff like ironing or the dishes. She doesn't watch much TV.

My aim is to reach Harry! I want to make a story so compelling that if Harry happens to channel surf onto the program I've made, he'll be so captivated, he'll not only watch with his mouth hanging open, but he'll also shout "Hey Martha, you gotta come and see this!" Martha comes running. Then you have what we call a "Hey Martha!" event. You have made an important breakthrough.

People have internal filtering systems to stop themselves going into "information overload".

The key thing of course is that Harry probably won't call for Martha because you've just updated the annual rainfall statistics for Burkina Faso [not that that isn't important], but you have to surprise him.

> **"Tell me something I don't know, and take me somewhere I've never been before."**

Getting Through the Filter

Now that we have entered the 21st century, we find ourselves in an information-saturated world. What we have learned in the last 15 years is the equivalent of what we learned in the fifteen centuries prior to that.

People have internal filtering systems to stop themselves going into "information overload". That means, as the multitude of images, words and ideas assaults their senses each day, much is discarded as irrelevant, if it doesn't affect them.

One commentator says we need to be discovering those things which people feel threatened by, are genuinely interested in, as new information, and there's a third thing – that which people value. Tapping into those subject areas will ensure that people sit up and take notice.

A current affairs producer told me early in my career about a personal maxim of his, for making great factual television. He said "Tell me something I don't know, and take me somewhere I've never been before." I have found his words to be incredibly useful in programme making and also in preaching.

I reckon that people sitting in church and listening to our messages often have the same kind of filtering systems in their hearts, as they have when they are watching television. They will discard the predictable, the too-general and the unimaginative. My aim in my speaking these days, is to produce "Hey-Martha" moments as often as I can, and also to take them places they've never been before.

> **Nathan broke through David's defences in a way that a "front-door" approach would probably not have achieved.**

Getting Under the Radar

So why use stories? And why are stories such an important part of what we actually remember from the pages of the Bible? Probably because, among other things, stories are a great way of getting people to understand the point you're making, by the sheer power of illustration.

The confronting of King David in the Bible about his adultery with Bathsheba, and his murderous attempts at cover-up, provides a great example of how the use of a story by the prophet Nathan, broke through David's defences in a way that a "front-door" approach would probably not have achieved.

Having slept with Bathsheba, and made her pregnant, David had tried to entice her husband Uriah home from war so he'd have sex with his wife and then believe the child was his own. When that plan didn't work, David arranged for Uriah to be killed in battle.

If Nathan had gone to David, throwing out the accusations in his first breath, it's likely that the King, having been so elaborate in his subterfuge, would have simply denied his offending.

Nathan was very wise. He told David a story.

It's telling stories in which people can suddenly see themselves and their actions in a new light.

There were two men in a certain town, one rich and the other poor. The rich man had a very large number of sheep and cattle, but the poor man had nothing except one little ewe lamb he had bought. He raised it, and it grew up with him and his children. It shared his food, drank from his cup, and even slept in his arms. It was like a daughter to him.

Now a traveller came to the rich man, but the rich man refrained from taking one of his own sheep or cattle to prepare a meal for the traveller. Instead, he took the ewe lamb that belonged to the poor man and prepared it for the one who had come to him.

David burned with anger against the man and said to Nathan, "As surely as the Lord lives, the man who did this deserves to die! He must pay for that lamb four times over, because he did such a thing and had no pity."
[2 Sam 12: 1-6]

Nathan's response is one of the most ringing phrases in all of scripture. Eyeballing one of the most powerful men on earth he said, "You are the man."

David was utterly undone by the story. It was as if he'd had the sheer awfulness of his crime painted in technicolour before his eyes. He owned up to what he'd done.

This is what we call "getting under the radar." It's telling stories in which people can suddenly see themselves and their actions in a new light.

But where does this leave us as storytellers? Are we supposed to sit back and wait for God to give us a great Nathan-style message? Is it OK to go out there and gather material? Does the use of too many modern stories or analogies blunt the impact of scripture or take us away from "sound doctrine?"

I don't want to suggest we give talks full of modern tales and devoid of scripture. Clearly both are valuable, when rightly used.

The Bible says David "shepherded them with integrity of heart; [and] with skilful hands he led them." [Psalm 78:72] Skill in speaking and integrity with God are great companion attributes and over the next few chapters, I want to build a case for a happy synergy between being great teachers of the Bible and great illustrators. Won't you join me?

–2–

The Pursuit of Excellence

"Do a little bit more than average, and from that point on, your progress multiplies itself out of all proportion to the effort put in."
–Paul J. Meyer

"Whatever you do, work at it with all your heart ..."
–Colossians 3:23

Is there anything wrong with excellence? Seems a strange question to have to ask, but over the years you hear so many sermons and talks that sound like they've just been thrown together, you start to wonder whether everyone believes our messages deserve blood, sweat and tears.

Working in television, an industry funded largely by advertising, you become aware how much care, time, energy and money goes into making a TV commercial. I recently interviewed an account manager for an ad agency, and he showed me the latest 60-second beer commercial he'd made. It had cost three quarters of a million dollars. And that was before it had even screened.

So I've always been amazed at how much care is taken over the selling of perishable stuff.

Dogfood and Shampoo

Some of the most creative minds in the world are engaged in what I call the "dog-food and shampoo" game. Some one has described this as the "use me, buy me, eat me, wear me, try me, drive me, put me in your hair" industry.

> **Some of the most creative minds in the world are engaged in what I call the "dogfood and shampoo" game.**

There are men and women in my home town who will stay up till three in the morning putting together a presentation based around predicting the kinds of cookies we'll be eating in five years' time.

> **The most important change, without a doubt, has been the development of television, transforming us into the most "visual" generation of all time.**

And they'll do that kind of brainstorming pretty regularly in the advertising industry. Sometimes, just to be a bit provocative I'll ask preachers when was the last time they stayed up till the wee small hours agonising over a key transition in a sermon. I know that's not the genuine mark of spirituality or diligence – but I do believe that devotion to excellence in the preparation of messages has a great payoff, as I hope to demonstrate.

I haven't set out to write a book on the finer points of hermeneutics, exposition or any other major area of scriptural interpretation, because those are not my specialty. There's no doubt that history proves the value of teaching and majoring in those areas.

What I'm passionate about is drawing people to the truth by imaginative application of story telling techniques, and the use of modern idiom in our preaching.

It's interesting to examine the philosophy of two great men of God from the 18th century, John and Charles Wesley, and how they adapted their methods to the British culture of their day. Writes one commentator:

"They agreed to become 'more vile'... and preach in the fields and town squares... in other words on the turf of unchurched people... They wrote Christian poetry to be sung to the tunes that people knew and people loved [pub music]... they created an architectural style for chapels in which common people would be comfortable. They coached Methodists to speak 'in the most obvious easy and common words wherein our meaning could be conveyed' and 'never to deviate from the most usual way of speaking'"[1]

A Visual Generation

What's happened, of course, is that things have not stood still since the days of the Wesley brothers, and the most important change, without a doubt, has been the development of television, transforming us into the most "visual" generation of all time.

People are no longer disposed to getting their information and their values by sitting in orderly rows.

Television has made a far greater impact than you'll ever know. What comes across our screens now has the power to touch us, engaging our senses, shaping our view on the world and in some cases chiseling our values.

Someone has observed that once upon a time the power bases in society were to be found in the universities, the church and the home. The advent of the so-called "global village" created by network and satellite TV means that the medium itself has become the university, the family, and the religion of many people.

I've been stunned on filming assignments in the most desperately poor slums of Asia, as I've walked through narrow lanes, where filth runs in the gutters, where people barely have enough to eat, where disease is rampant. But all the while, behind the grimy curtains you catch its sight and sound: the faint blue glow of the TV screen, and the glazed eyes of those who seem to sit and watch entranced, for hours on end.

In the West the changes we have been through mean that people are no longer disposed to getting their information and their values by sitting in orderly rows listening to someone stand behind a lectern for 30 to 45 minutes at a time. What's more you, as a preacher, are no longer the most educated and influential person in your town.

Add to this trend, the effect of television on people's attention spans – about six seconds before a child's mind will wander, for adults about eight seconds – and you see the potential for boring messages and distractions to derail listeners' thought processes away from what you are saying.

The implication is clear: to teach people well, we need to be great communicators and one way to achieve this is to be great storytellers, and paint the most vivid pictures we can for our listeners.

What Kinds of Stories?

> **Jesus didn't tell "religious stories," as such. He told tales about birds and flowers and coins and nets and fig trees.**

There's no end to the kinds of stories you can find and use. I am going to suggest a wide range of possibilities as we go along, But for starters, you might choose:
- a story or episode from your own experience
- a story you've found and read
- something from today's newspaper which you describe and from which you might draw a lesson
- a modern parable you have written all by yourself
- a Bible story, retold or updated, with flair and imagination

Does this mean I am saying that Bible stories alone are no longer the best way to teach Biblical truth? By no means. Later in the book I will cover a range of ideas to help you bring Bible stories to life in even more compelling ways.

But in the meantime I am suggesting there is a vital role for the power of the modern parable, analogy and illustration. Remember: Jesus didn't tell "religious stories," as such. He told tales about birds and flowers and coins and nets and fig trees. He used images, ideas and experiences of his time to connect with his listeners.

So, be realistic about who you're talking to. David Pearce from the Christian rock group "No Longer Music" cities a great example of this. When the band toured in Europe, he found many modern city-dwelling kids, in towns like Amsterdam, had virtually zero experience of what happens on farms.

> **No great novel or movie ever gives away the whole plot in the first scene.**

This meant, that the classic Sheep and Shepherd stories were probably still valid – but only up to a point. Pearce found that when he applied his mind to finding analogies that connected more incisively with a highly urbanised audience, it paid off in terms of understanding.

Thinking Differently

So where do we start? I want to suggest at the beginning, that there is great benefit in a little subtlety. No great novel or movie ever gives away the whole plot in the first scene.

As we paint our word pictures for our listeners, think about the element of surprise. This is sometimes called "tension and release." Remember how the real sting in Nathan's story got underneath David's "radar" by touching his heart?

Skilled speakers understand this principle and know how an audience can be reached by drawing them into scenes that initially seem to have little bearing to the talk subject, but which will later prove to have powerful relevance.

Take the subject of abortion for example. Highly emotive, and in one sense, difficult to tackle with anything other than a head-on approach and a bunch of grim statistics.

Bill Hybels, senior pastor at Willow Creek Community Church in Chicago, had another idea. In his series called "Our Modern Moral Trifecta," here's how he starts a talk on abortion.

Well, my friends said that I would never forget it. I was about ten years old. I had gotten a BB gun for my birthday, and they said, "You ought to go out and shoot a bird. You'll never forget it."

I'd never hunted anything in my life. So I took that brand new BB gun and I stalked birds around our property. Finally I saw a robin – state bird of Michigan. They throw you in jail if you mess with them, but I thought, there's no way I'm going to hit this robin.

So I drew a bead on it, I pulled the trigger and I hit it. But it wasn't like they said it was going to be. It didn't just keel over and die. It flew a little ways in a very contorted way. Then it flopped around on the ground. It was chirping and screaming. It was bleeding and it looked very unnatural.

A talk, which comes straight out of left field – a personal take on life and death at the very outset.

As I stood over it, looking at what I had done, I couldn't believe it. When that struggling, bleeding bird finally died, I ran to my room and closed the door, fell on the bed and cried. I didn't like that.

Some years ago, a guy in my small group died. There were four of us men in this group who walked together in relationship for about ten years. One of the guys in the group got a brain tumour and died.

When we knew he was close to the end, we got the phone call and we raced to the hospital. He died in his room while we were in the lobby. But we all went up anyway. For a while we were granted the privilege of standing at the foot of his bed while he lay there dead. The three of us silently cursed the one who steals life away. Then we went across the street, the three of us remaining members of that group. We sat in a Burger King until one guy finally said "I hate death."[2]

In this way, Hybels sets up a talk which comes straight out of left field – a personal take on life and death at the very outset. He gets a sense of identification from his audience, because these experiences are likely to resonate powerfully with many of his listeners.

He then builds effectively into a message, which asks listeners to contemplate some of the anomalies in a world where life is sacred once outside the womb, but vulnerable and risky when one rewinds the video of that infant's life by "a few frames".

Coming Into the Here and Now

Another great story telling technique, which I'll cover in more detail in later chapters, is all about painting new pictures with Bible stories. I don't think God ever intended that every parable or scriptural illustration would only be effective unless it's read word for word in Elizabethan English!

The truth is, the stories Jesus told are incredibly powerful. And without trying to sound heretical, there are occasions when those stories, brought into modern scenarios, then have fresh life and relevance injected into them.

Eventually after enough books not read and games not played they stop complaining. Because they stop expecting.

John Ortberg, teaching pastor at Willow Creek Community Church has done this kind of thing brilliantly over many years. In a memorable talk entitled "It all goes back in the box," Ortberg takes the well-known story Jesus told about the rich barn builder, and brings it firmly into the present day.

The Busy Guy's Story

This is the story of a busy guy. He was committed and he was willing to do whatever it would take to make his earthly dreams come true.

And it would take everything.

So he finds himself consumed by his work. An entrepreneur, he puts in 12 – 14 hour days, works weekends, joins professional organisations and boards of directors to expand his contacts.

And even when he's not working he finds his mind drifting towards work, so that work becomes not just his occupation, but his preoccupation.

His wife often tries to slow him down – to remind him that he has a family; and vaguely he's aware of the fact that his kids are growing up, and he's missing it, and from time to time they complain about books they want him to read or games of catch they want to play. But eventually after enough books not read and games not played they stop complaining. Because they stop expecting.

And he says to himself that he'll become more available to the important people of his life – in six months or so, when things settle down. It's one of his favourite phrases – when things settle down.

This guy is like a man consumed, and every waking moment is devoted to this once in a lifetime opportunity.

And although he's a very bright guy, this man in Jesus' story, he never seems to notice the fact that things never settle down.

"Anyway", he says to himself when he feels guilty, "I'm doing it all for them".

He wakes up at one o'clock one morning, and he feels this twinge in his chest, and his wife makes an appointment with the doctor and they tell him he's actually had a slight heart attack. They warn him all the symptoms are there – elevated blood pressure, cholesterol levels etc, and he's got to make some changes in his life.

And for a while he does. He starts working on his health, he gets into an exercise programme, watches what he eats, less Rocky Roads and so on, but when the symptoms go away, so does his motivation for change. He says to himself, "I just don't have time to do all that stuff". He says "I'll get around to it, when things settle down."

He recognises that his life is out of balance.

His wife tries to get him to go to church with her, and he intends to do it, but when Sunday morning rolls around, it feels to him like that's the only time in the week when he can crash, besides he says the church is so big and getting in there and parking is such a hassle.

And he says, "I can believe without the church; there'll be time for that, when things settle down."

One day the head of his company comes to him and says, "You're not going to believe this, but business is booming such that we can barely keep up with it. We're on the brink of a miracle, this is our chance to strike the motherlode and if we catch this wave we'll be set for life. But it's going to take major changes."

From this moment this guy is like a man consumed, and every waking moment is devoted to this once in a lifetime opportunity.

And that night he goes home to his wife, and he's all excited and he says, "You know what this means, don't you? Once I get through with this project, we can relax. Our future will be assured, we'll be set for life, because I know the market, I've covered every base, I've anticipated every eventuality. We will finally have financial security, be able to take those vacations you've always wanted and so on."

But she'd heard that song before and she'd learned not to get her hopes up.

At eleven o'clock that night she says, "I'm going to bed, you want to come up with me?

He says," I'll be there in a few minutes, I've got a little more work I want to do, but you go ahead and I'll be there in a few minutes."

Three o'clock in the morning she wakes up and she's alone in bed and he's still not there. She says, "This is ridiculous!" She goes downstairs to drag him up, and he's still sitting at the table in front of the terminal. His head's resting on the table, and she says to herself, "It's like being married to a child – he would rather fall asleep down here than come up to bed." And she touches him on the shoulder to wake him, but he doesn't respond and his skin is cold to her touch.

She goes to the phone and she dials for an ambulance, a panicky feeling in the pit of her stomach, but by the time the paramedics get there, they check him out, and tell her he's had a massive heart attack and he's been dead for hours.

His death is a major story in the financial community. His obituary is written up in all the big journals, and it's too bad he was dead, because he would have loved to have read what they wrote about him. And then they had this memorial service for him. The

It's too bad he was dead, because he would have loved to have read what they wrote about him.

Some people are so busy making a living that they don't have time to make a life.

whole community comes to it, and they all file past his casket, and they all make the same stupid comment that people always make at funerals: "He looks so peaceful." Rigor mortis will do that to a person!

People get up to eulogise him. He's been one of the leading entrepreneurs of the day. One of them says, "He was an innovator in technology and delivery systems."

Says another: "He was a man of principle." Someone else says, "He was a straight arrow guy, he would never cheat."

Another person says, "He had all kinds of civic achievements, he was a pillar in his community, he knew everybody, he was a networker."

And then they all got together and they had a memorial constructed for him and they wrote inspiring words on it – words that they would choose to try to summarise his life. Entrepreneur, innovator, leader, visionary, pillar, success. And they buried him and they put up the memorial and they all went home.

But then when it was dark, and there was no-one around to observe, then unseen, unheard, came the angel of God, to this cemetery and made his way through all of the graves to the grave of this man and there traced with a finger the single word that God chose to summarise the meaning of this man's life. You know what the word was? Fool.

"You fool," God said. "For all of your financial acumen, for all of your ability to run cost benefit analyses, and cash flow projections, there was one scenario you forgot."

You know what it was? It was death. He forgot to consider the possibility that somewhere along the line that he might die.

And God stands amazed at the folly of a human being who painstakingly prepares for every contingency, covers the bases of every eventuality – however unlikely – and forgets the one inevitable certainty that stares every one of us in the face from the moment we are born, which is,that we're going to die.

Some people are so busy making a living that they don't have time to make a life. [3]

■■■■■

What I love so much about teaching like this, is that it's the kind of talk you could hear as a seeker, or a believer of forty years, and still be deeply and effectively taught, no matter which camp you're in. Sometimes you hear people observe that it's not really possible to reach both seekers and believers in an optimal way in one kind of church service. I'm inclined to believe it is at least possible to do it very often, if we give care and attention to our messages.

Never underestimate the value of teaching – especially to the unchurched – by creative means.

Talking With Pictures

Another feature of storytelling is the concept of taking the visual elements of your message, and being even bolder – by integrating things like drama and visual props into the overall message.

Never underestimate the value of teaching – especially to the unchurched – by creative means. A few years back, a Christian wife with a stubbornly resistant husband, finally got him into church. He'd fought hard for ages against her beliefs, saying that he expected to hear nothing from a preacher that would have relevance to his fast paced role in the business world.

That morning, members of the church drama group performed a sketch some of you may have seen. It's about a guy who's so busy trying to keep a bunch of plates spinning atop poles on the stage, he eventually runs out of hands, and loses the plate-spinning battle.

The more of a listener's senses you can engage in the process, the more effective you can sometimes be.

Midway through the sketch our tough, resistant business type turns to his wife with tears in his eyes, and nods and says, "Yeah, that's my life." The more you think about it, that guy got well and truly ministered to that morning.

"How?" you might ask. Well, someone just enlivened that passage from Ecclesiastes that speaks of "better one handful with tranquility than two handfuls with toil and chasing after the wind." [Ecclesiastes 4:6] The scripture had been brought to life for that man.

Are there other ways of doing this kind of thing creatively? You bet! And the more of a listener's senses you can engage in the process, the more effective you can sometimes be.

The Power of What We See

Why should this be? It's a principle Jesus obviously understood extremely well. He'd place a little child in the midst of the disciples and tell them that in order to be great in the Kingdom of Heaven, they needed to become childlike.

He'd ask for a coin, hold it up and ask whose image was on the coin, in order to teach the difference between earthly and heavenly allegiances. So much of His teaching was rich in illustration.

A major research project conducted at UCLA found that many teachers probably have a completely unrealistic idea about how effective they're being as communicators by underestimating the visual elements of teaching.

Professor Albert Mehrabian found that when it comes to believability, the actual "word content" of a spoken presentation has relatively little to do with the overall impression you make as a speaker.

Researching what makes a speaker believable, he found there were three key factors: verbal [what the speaker says], vocal [how the presentation sounds] and visual [what the listener sees as the presentation is being given]. Someone has called these the three V's of spoken communication.

The results, when it came to percentages, were quite astonishing.

Person after person did serious business with God that morning.

Verbal was just seven percent, vocal contributed 38 percent, and visual impression was a huge 55 percent. In other words, imagining that listeners or an audience or a congregation are just like computer terminals, ready to receive raw, downloaded information, is a fallacy.

Now clearly, there are limits to this kind of research, and far be it from me to rule out the role of the Spirit of God, moving over a preacher's words and touching listeners in His sovereign way. But you sometimes have the feeling, there are preachers who reckon everything is going to be put right by the Holy Spirit – even a lack of care in talk preparation, and a speaking technique that could do with some attention!

But I digress! The point I am really trying to make, is that on the occasions when a chance to "get visual" presents itself – take it! And sometimes you can get really creative.

Casting Stones

I heard of one preacher's take on the story from John 8 about the woman they brought before Jesus, after having caught her in the act of adultery. You know the deal: they were going to put her to death, and Jesus challenged them to stone her, only once they were completely satisfied they were sinless themselves.

The stone carriers and the stony-faced religious types all melted away at that challenge, leaving Jesus alone with the woman, and extending his hand of grace and a second chance.

The modern-day preacher handed out big round stones at the door as people came in for his sermon. A good-sized rock in every hand coming into church that day.

"Feel the weight of it," the preacher exhorted, once everyone was seated and listening. "Make a nice dent in someone wouldn't it!" Then he encouraged them to think about unresolved anger, about secret bitterness, about people in the lives of the listeners who they felt probably deserved the verbal or emotional equivalent of a rock between the eyes.

Then he quietly took them to the next step. "So how about it?" he asked, a bit like Jesus had 2000 years earlier. "How about making today the day you lay down your rock, that heavy thing you've been carrying, not so much in your hands, but in your heart? How about bringing that rock up here this morning, right to the foot of the cross, and finding the strength to lay it down?"

The effect, as you can well imagine, was quite electrifying, as person after person did serious business with God that morning, and a steadily growing pile of rocks, some stained with fresh tears, built around the cross on the stage.

If you think it's worth the risk of handing out rocks to a couple of hundred people one Sunday just before you preach, don't you get a sense it might just be a pretty powerful exercise?

It really is all about bringing those great truths of the Bible into the here and now.

–3–

Everyone Has A Story

*"I have always believed... that whatever good or bad fortune
may come our way we can always give it meaning and
transform it into something of value."*

–Herman Hesse

Great storytellers are an inspiration to both TV reporters and preachers alike. Steve Hartman, an American current affairs correspondent is one of my personal favourites.

For several years, he used an amazing technique to decide who next to interview for his character profiles: he'd get someone to throw a dart at a big map of the country, then go to the spot, however obscure, and then find a number in the local phone directory, with a random stab of his own finger. Whoever answered the phone, would become his next story!

The results were stunning, and proved the truth of the contention that everyone has a tale worth telling, and worth hearing.

Everyone has a tale worth telling, and worth hearing.

One very funny and moving story from Northern Tennessee concerned a five year old boy called Trey Pyles, who couldn't keep still in church. Any parent could identify with the squirming, irritable boy who kept asking when it was going to be time to go home.

But Steve discovered a gem in Trey's life story. Once every few weeks, Trey liked to go see his Grandma. The camera shows Trey collecting a helium filled balloon, a bright green one, from a store, then heading with his mum into the countryside to see Grandma.

At the top of a hill, above a picturesque valley, you start to see where the story's going. It's great tension and release. Grandma, we learn, is dead, and the five-year-old – instead of taking flowers to a grave, wants to give her something she can grasp.

Here's how Steve's script brilliantly wraps it all up.

Trey used to see his Grandma nearly every day. He was two when she died, and yet he clearly still remembers.

I asked Trey how you would give a balloon to someone who's not here any more and he obliged, but didn't take me to the cemetery. Because his way of thinking is, why tie it to a tombstone when she's not even there? Why not bring up here [onto the hilltop] and let her catch it?

As Trey watched that balloon disappear into his Grandma's arms, I realised that he did have something to say, after all, that faith is where you find it, and that there's a lot more to religion that just sitting up straight on Sundays.[1]

People Watching

Like Steve Hartman, you can be a watcher of people, and discover that great stories, and real life parables are everywhere. As you travel about, don't be afraid to ask questions of those among whom you mingle. Nearly everyone you meet has a story worth storing away.

I've heard lots of stories about how Martin Luther King came to coin those powerful words "I Have A Dream," which became part of perhaps the most well-known speech of the twentieth century. Who knows for sure, exactly which version is true? I heard one that sounded pretty good!

In a documentary on King's life, one of his co-workers from the early days in Alabama, Dorothy Cotton, gives a fascinating insight into how King listened carefully, everywhere he went, gathering material for his talks. [2]

"Dr King could see a sermon in so many places and in so many things."

Recalls Cotton: "I heard one of the white

girls saying in this little church, that 'I have a dream one day that my child,' and she points to a black woman sitting there, 'can reach out and hold hands with your child some day, and it won't matter.' "

Cotton goes on: "This girl had just made a wonderful remark about her dream as a white woman. Dr King could see a sermon in so many places and in so many things." Dorothy then describes in the programme how she related the story of the woman's dream to King. The rest is history.

"I have a dream that one day, down in Alabama... one day right there in Alabama, little black boys and black girls will be able to join hands with little white boys and white girls as sisters and brothers, I have a dream today!"

Even if the story's only partly true, it gives powerful testimony to the notion that listening to stories can lead to great presentations!

Just Looking!

There'd be very few of us who'd consider ourselves as being in the same league as Martin Luther King, but we can all be good listeners and story-tellers.

It probably pales a bit, alongside the ringing phrases of King's great speeches, but let me just share a few thoughts from personal experience along these lines.

Perhaps it might help if I describe over the next few pages, some of the astonishing people I have met during my career as a journalist and TV producer, and tell you what they taught me and how I used my observations as teaching material.

Many of these stories have been used in a radio outreach series called "Scrubcutters" – 90 second inserts prepared by the Christian Broadcasting Association of New Zealand. So, many of my stories are designed to be a self contained lesson that can be broadcast in a minute and a half slot between traffic reports and news bulletins.

The idea is to connect with a listening audience in a very short space of time. My point in sharing these tales, is to get you thinking about the people you meet and the experiences you have, as potential teaching material. Here are a few, with portions added in some cases.

Child Number 30

A few years ago I was finishing up a filming assignment for the aid agency Opportunity International, in Ghana.

We'd spent most of our time filming around a town in the interior, called Kumasi. Opportunity International has a base there, employing quite a few local people to administer the system of so-called Trustbanks – a brilliant way of providing low interest loans to poor people so they can start businesses and support their families. It's all underpinned by strong Christian values and a system of business mentoring, which goes along with the loans.

Daniel, our Ghanaian driver on the trip really interested me, because on every one of the four days we'd been with him – he'd always looked immaculate in the African heat. Shirt pressed, trousers with a sharp crease – not a hair out of place.

This was in stark contrast to my own appearance after each day's filming. I looked like a wrung out dishrag! I was doubly impressed with Daniel because on our last day of filming we stopped by his house. I'd describe it as a mud hut with a tin roof.

"How does a guy come out of a mud hut each day, looking like a Pierre Cardin clothing model?" I wondered.

But Daniel had more surprises in store. How many brothers and sisters, I asked. "Twenty-nine," he said quietly, but then added "Of course, my Dad has eight wives."

"He's recently become a Christian," Daniel told me. "Now he's cutting down – he just has four wives." Unique pastoral challenge I thought, as I spared a thought for the four wives who were maybe out on the street now!

Turns out that Daniel, at 26, was the youngest of the thirty kids. And Dad's by no means a rich man, as the humble hut indicated. But here's what really impressed me: I asked Daniel if he hoped to progress from working in a lowly position in the local aid agency office. Perhaps he might make manager one day, I joked.

"Oh no," said Daniel seriously. As we drove on, I felt a moment's panic – had I offended him? But he went on… "I've saved enough money, and next month I'm going to a college in America, where I'm going to get

> **Gather those tales, and retain the details as you learn about them.**

my masters, then my PHD, then ultimately I'm going to establish and head up a brand new aid organisation, to bring dignity, jobs and help to people all across Africa. That's my ten-year plan," he said.

My head was reeling; not only does child number thirty not feel sorry for himself, he irons his clothes in a mud hut every morning, then gets out and says "World, bring it on! I'm going to make a difference."

Daniel loves his God, anguishes for his people and dares to dream big every day. He truly inspired me, and I determined to keep in touch with him. About a year later, I checked with him by email. Sure enough, his studies in Alabama are going well. I have no doubt he'll realise his dreams.

■■■■■

I tend to tell Daniel's story a lot. It has great elements of humour, some "Hey Martha" factor and it helps bring great perspective. So often, in the West, we major on fretting over the limitations we see in our lives, while the Daniels of this world feed their hearts on the good, the honourable and the praiseworthy promises of God and make a huge difference.

To gather the 'Daniel' stories, I reckon a notebook is an indispensable tool for a professional storyteller. Gather those tales, and retain the details as you learn about them.

In story telling, I believe it's helpful if some of your "people stories" can help you slaughter some sacred cows along the way.

We're so hung up on cramming words down people's throats sometimes. Every now and then you meet someone who can help you make powerful points about how love and effectiveness are found in surprising places, in ways that don't involve great oratory that goes on for hours. Here's an example you may find helpful.

The Clown

One of the best communicators I ever saw in action never spoke a single word. And yet, he managed to teach his audience lessons which went on to save some lives.

His name was Aaron Ward, a 26 year old from Auckland, New Zealand. Aaron went to refugee camps on the borders of Kosovo, to bring joy and laughter to kids whose lives had been turned upside down by the cruel war and mass deportations which shattered that country in 1999.

Turns out Aaron, who worked part-time as a clown, had been watching those awesome TV pictures we all saw – that mass eviction, that ethnic cleansing at the hands of Milosevic's army. He was so moved in his safe, cosy world in New Zealand, he started calling up aid agencies and offering his services free of charge.

"I was desperate to do something," Aaron recalls. "I naively assumed that the first people I rang would instantly see the value of sending a clown to the borders of Kosovo. But no one really wanted to know. I think they thought logistics experts and engineers and nurses would be of more use."

But eventually, someone in World Vision caught the idea.

"They reckoned they could use me as a psychosocial worker," Aaron recalls now with a smile. "That made sense to the UN and the others who were initially dubious about the concept of me clowning my way round the Balkans."

So off went Aaron, with his clown gear in his bag, to the miserable refugee camps where the Albanians who'd been thrown out of Kosovo, were living in squalid, desperate conditions.

Aaron would dress up as a clown – a clown he called Elvo. This clown did everything in silence – miming his messages. The photos World Vision got back from the camps in Macedonia and Montenegro said it all. Children who'd seen their relatives killed and their homes destroyed, smiling again, for the first time.

As I traveled with Aaron/Elvo the following year back into Kosovo, to renew friendships with youngsters who'd met him when they were refugees, I was deeply moved.

Not only were the children thrilled to see the clown who'd made them laugh in the midst of their pain and dislocation, but they also came with amazing stories.

Elvo had shown them in the camps, in a powerful, yet wordless skit, how to avoid being injured by landmines – the deadly farewell presents left by the retreating Serb army in Kosovo.

Now, the kids and their parents were coming back with grateful tales of how children had found mines – and instead of exercising their curiosity and playing with the devices, they'd recalled the clown's skit, and had run back to the villages to summon a mine clearance expert.

World Vision, who used Aaron's skills in the region, estimates that scores of lives and limbs have been saved by the creative teaching.

I saw first hand a great truth about communication: it is not about what the teacher teaches, but what the learner learns. It was also a timely reminder about how weary the world becomes of people who just throw out words, without corresponding actions and love.

■ ■ ■ ■ ■

Hunting and Collecting

In your notebook, make sure you collect those fascinating tidbits that other people tell you have also had a profound effect on their lives. If you can remember at the time, see if you can get permission to use those stories.

I'll often say to someone who's told me of a very moving personal experience, "Look, I find that story incredibly powerful. I talk to groups of people quite often, and I think others would benefit greatly from the lessons you just told me you'd learned."

People are usually thrilled – provided the story's not too embarrassing – and it's much better to seek permission. It's a small world, and things get back to people!

Here's what I did with a story I heard from a flight attendant, for a very short radio piece I wanted to do about Christian involvement.

Flying Over Timor

This age we're living in brings with it, a curious mixture of closeness and detachment. A flight attendant I know, told me of the bizarre contradictions she experiences, in the first class section of the planes on which she works.

She told me about flying over East Timor at 37,000 feet, right at the time the awful struggles were taking place there, as the nation sought independence.

It was time to pour another glass of vintage Chardonnay for a traveller, whose thoughts soon turned to other, more pleasant musings.

"From that height," she said, "We could see the smoke from the fires below and could only imagine the awful things happening beneath us."

Passengers and crew were all a bit glum for a little while, she told me, but then, it was time to pour another glass of vintage

Chardonnay for a traveller, whose thoughts soon turned to other, more pleasant musings.

Her story really made me think. Lest I sound cynical, let me go on to say that I believe this curious proximity to pain which we sometimes experience, does have its upsides. The media, for example, with all its foibles, at least has the ability to bring great need right into our living rooms or to our ears, virtually as it's happening.

The Ethiopian famine of the mid eighties is a classic example. When we finally shouted. "Enough!" highly imaginative rescue projects like Band Aid took off, with amazing results.

The key of course is found in stories like the Good Samaritan. The message? If you see pain, don't pass by and assume it's too hard to fix. The Samaritan made the difference in that story because he came near to where the suffering man was – had compassion and got his hands dirty as he brought healing and relief.

It is still what the one who told that story would have us do.

■■■■■

The account from the flight attendant gave me a slightly bizarre, but nonetheless hopefully interesting way to give a new twist to an old truth – with the particular aim of reaching a partially secular radio audience.

Sometimes you find yourself right in the middle of what becomes a powerful parable. I had such an experience a few years ago when I went traveling with a man I'll never forget.

Desperately Seeking Diana

Alan's Routley's daughter Diana had gone missing while backpacking in India in the summer of 1997. She was an experienced traveler, who regularly kept in touch with the folks back home in New Zealand.

Diana was a bright and bubbly 26 year old, who had flown from London

Find the stories, which resonate with your listeners, on levels they can understand.

to New Delhi, but had then failed to emerge from the ancient pilgrim city of Varanasi.

Diana's disappearance spurred Alan into action. "I was straight up with my other children," says Alan. "I had been successful in my job and my bank balance was healthy. But I told the kids that if it took every last cent of their inheritance, I would keep looking till I found their sister."

When I picked up the story, Alan had been trying desperately to get information out of India, but to no avail. So he went to India himself. He took with him hundreds of posters with Diana's photo and details on, printed in Hindi and English, which he intended to put up in hostels and hotels all over the subcontinent.

When I met up with Alan in Varanasi, it was his second trip there. I filmed as he scoured the narrow alleyways in 40-degree heat, wandered along the banks of the Ganges, and pestered the local police for any news of Diana.

The final outcome was awful and tragic. Police found the remains of the young Auckland girl, buried in a crude grave under a house where she'd been murdered by greedy men who'd stolen her travellers cheques. There's been a murder trial: it's still unresolved as I write, and for Diana's family, there'll always be a huge sense of loss.

I guess what struck me was the sheer determination and restlessness of one father, who wouldn't give up till he knew what had happened to his girl. Right till the time they found Diana's grave, Alan still clung to any shred of hope he could muster: maybe, just maybe she was alive somewhere. He wouldn't give up till he was sure there was no chance.

To have someone prepared to go the ends of earth to find us and rescue us from the things that hurt us, is at the heart of what makes us civilized, and is the central truth of the Christian message.

Our Heavenly Father has billions of "missing children." Throughout the universe, I guess you could imagine the posters with those faces on, as a loving Dad pines for these kids to come home.

In the end, by sending Jesus, that lovesick Father shows us that he's prepared to spare nothing to get us back, to exhaust every possibility to show us that he loves us and wants to be in eternal relationship with us.

■■■■■

My advice? Find the stories which resonate with your listeners, on levels they can understand. Jesus did this kind of teaching all the time. To teach deep and profound truths about God, he would appeal to their understanding of human relationships.

"If your little boy asks for a serving of fish, do you scare him with a live snake on his plate? If your little girl asks for an egg, do you trick her with a spider? As bad as you are, you wouldn't think of such a thing – you're at least decent to your own children. And don't you think the Father who conceived you will give the Holy Spirit when you ask him?"
–Luke 11: 11-13 [THE MESSAGE]

What Jesus did was simply ask, "Any Dads here?" then taught about God in ways that they could feel as well as comprehend. But there's even more potential in the power of example, as we're about to see.

—4—

Provocation by Example

"You can preach a better sermon with your life than with your lips."
—Oliver Goldsmith

"I want to test the sincerity of your love by comparing it with the earnestness of others."
—2 Corinthians 8:8

Living a more honourable or more sacrificial life is a lot like dieting; great in theory, much tougher in practice. Those of us who've tried to raise other people's game or lift their performance by preaching at them, have all experienced the glazed looks that come back at you when you talk in generalities about "doing better", "raising the bar", or "taking the next hill".

People often find it hard to imagine lifting their performance in the abstract. It's also extremely frustrating for a listener to simply hear broad and imprecise encouragements to live sacrificially or overcome more hurdles, if the speaker lacks focus or examples.

This is where storytelling really comes into its own. People who are facing hardship or who are cynical about the prospects of improving their life really need to hear how others have done exactly what is being asked of them. Especially if listeners have been embittered by tragedy, loss or betrayal, they tend to filter much of what they hear, through their past pains and may well conclude that the preacher knows little about real hurt.

A pastor of one of America's most successful and fast growing churches cottoned onto this reality early in his ministry and made an intriguing decision: to place no-one in a position of ministry, especially a preaching position, unless that person had experienced "some pain" in their life.

He clearly didn't want ministers who were out of touch with the real needs and hurts of ordinary people, and the success of his church has proved his instincts right. He'll often help illustrate one of his own sermons by bringing to the stage, right in the middle of the address, someone whose personal journey can poignantly validate what he's just said about a major issue.

Letting Them Tell Their Own Stories

When this technique is used properly it can make for some powerful messages. My wife Ali came home from a church service she'd been visiting a few years ago and told me she'd just heard one of the most insightful presentations of her life. She said the pastor brought to the platform a woman whose husband had recently committed suicide, and then conducted a 20-minute interview with her about the pain of her loss as a wife, mother and also as a Christian.

That brief interview provided a springboard into a fairly short talk the pastor then gave about how we as Christians ought to respond to those who've suffered major loss. Ali said it was some of the smartest communication she'd heard, made so much more relevant by the fact that a "real" person had shared their journey and showed that in spite of the pain, there was a way through. The pastor's message deconstructed many of the myths that surround suicide, loss and the process of grieving.

> **Survival is possible even in the midst of unimaginable hurt.**

Ali and I later learned that a number of people actually joined the church that morning saying things like "if a church has got the guts to confront this sort of issue in such an imaginative and caring way this is where I want to be."

This leads me to the real point of this chapter. You're onto a winner if you're able to find and relate real stories about people who've come through great pain and trial, having learned something, having grown, and having shown that survival is possible even in the midst of unimaginable hurt.

What's more, these stories by no means all have to be about great all-conquering Christians. Guts and bravery have a value all of their own and are worthy of using as a platform from which to teach broader spiritual principles.

Mike's Journey

A few years ago I met a man whose life journey is a case in point. I met Mike Reynolds in Fresno, California in the late 1990's. I was in the United States making a documentary about alternatives in the process of sentencing criminals.

Mike had a story of unique personal agony and loss, but the story had an ending, which was quite astounding. Mike and his wife had three great kids. The youngest of the three was their daughter, Kimber. She decided when she was 18 years old to leave Fresno and go several hundred miles south to Los Angeles to study the fashion business.

"She was my sweetheart, the apple of my eye," Mike told me. "Every time she'd come back up to visit from L.A, I'd make whatever excuse I could to keep her an extra day or two – offer to fix her car for her, anything to have her stick around with her Mum and me, we just loved her so much." On a return visit to her Mum and Dad's home in 1992, Kimber spent her last night in Fresno out at a restaurant with some friends. When she'd finished her meal she and the others stepped out into the street. What happened next really only lasted a matter of seconds but it felt like an eternity for those watching.

Two men pulled up next to the group on a powerful motorcycle. The man on the back of the bike snarled at Kimber and demanded that she hand over her purse. She was a feisty girl and flat out refused. Without hesitation the man pulled out a large calibre handgun and shot Kimber in the head at point blank range.

Kimber survived for twenty hours and slowly passed away on her hospital bed surrounded by family and friends. The tragedy for the Reynolds family was unimaginable, but what made it that much worse was the knowledge that the men on the motorcycle had both been recently released from prison on early parole after having been convicted of violent offences.

Mike Reynolds admits that for the first couple of weeks he didn't know whether he wanted to go on living or not. But when he began to emerge from the haze, he steeled himself and organised an unusual barbecue at his home. He invited local policemen, judges, social workers and anybody else he could imagine would be able to help him make sense of what had happened.

What emerged from that meeting at the Reynolds home was a very controversial idea. A plan to get the state of California to pass laws which would ensure that violent offenders were locked up for longer periods of time.

"I knew I just had to do something which would go some way to ensuring that another Dad didn't have to endure the pain that I'd been through," Mike told me. "Think of yourself as a father, with your child staring down the barrel of loaded gun. You'd do just about anything to avoid that child getting hurt, wouldn't you?"

What came of that initial barbecue at Mike Reynolds' place is now pretty legendary. A proposed new law would be put before the people of California at the next state ballot.

> **"I just had to do something which would go some way to ensuring that another Dad didn't have to endure the pain that I'd been through."**

The law would be called "Three Strikes And You're Out". Broadly speaking it would mean that if you'd had two previous convictions involving violence, on conviction of a third offence you'd go to prison for something between 25 years to life. The rationale was simple: to avoid people like the man who'd murdered Kimber Reynolds, being out on the street.

There was huge debate in California over the proposed law, but Mike Reynolds was resolute. "The groundswell of support was just staggering," says Mike. "I was running low on money, and I'd pull into a gas station. Someone would recognise me from the newspaper stories about Three Strikes and would thrust a couple of $20 bills into my hand to pay for my gas."

But the personal cost for Mike of trying to get the law passed was becoming consider-able. As they approached the critical date for the California referendum, Mike realised that the small pot of savings he'd built up from his job as a wedding photographer had dwindled to almost nothing, and the effort of going on the road to promote the new law had meant a huge amount of time away from his business with a consequential loss of earnings.

Only a few people in this life are privileged enough to get the chance to make sacrifices that can really result in other people's lives being saved.

It was a critical point in the campaign. Mike sensed that it was going to take one big last push, to get the Three Strikes law introduced. With his money almost out, Mike spent a restless night tossing and turning and then in the morning told his wife what he wanted to do.

"We had a little piece of land up in the mountains," recalls Mike. "I used to take Kimber and the boys up there for holidays in the summer, and I'd dreamed that one day I'd build a small cabin there." Mike told his wife he believed that only a few people in this life are privileged enough to get the chance to make sacrifices that can really result in other people's lives being saved. She nodded in agreement.

Within a short time Mike had sold the land in the mountains and used the money to print hundreds of thousands of leaflets and buy advertising space urging his fellow Californians to vote for the law.

The ballot saw the Three Strikes proposition passed into law. The implications of the law were as major as everybody had been predicting: lots of people locked up for very long periods of time upon their third strike.

But however controversial the law may have been, in the year following its introduction, the rate of murder, rape and robbery went down in California quite remarkably. "It was the first major drop in those awful statistics in more than a decade," says Mike proudly. "One policeman told me he reckoned there were hundreds of people whose lives had been saved and whose health and property had been protected because of the new law."

Mike had a deep belief that some sacrifices are really worthwhile.

The state of California later went on to modify the law because it was perceived to have some serious anomalies, but whatever the outcome, finally Mike Reynolds believed that he had been true to Kimber's memory and had at least, for a brief period of time, made a huge difference to crime statistics in his state.

Giving It All Away

When I met Mike and conducted an interview for our TV programme he had just made another major sacrifice. Not content to stop with Three Strikes, Mike had become a campaigner against the out-of-control availability of handguns in California.

Knowing that an illegal gun had caused the death of his daughter and knowing that guns were a feature of hundreds of thousands of other crimes, he set out to try and make it tougher for people to continue to commit crimes with these weapons. He'd proposed a brand new law, which he believed would do the job. Once again, his funds had almost run dry. He had one last beloved possession left. It was a beautiful, loving-ly maintained Chevrolet Corvette.

"I used to love that thing like a baby," says Mike with a big smile. "Used to almost kiss it goodnight in the evenings and polished it till it gleamed." But again, Mike had a deep belief that some sacrifices are really worth-while. He sold the car and on the day I visited him he'd once again turned the proceeds of the sale into scores of thousands of leaflets he was inserting in newspapers all over the State. Into his old van, he was load-ing the boxes of leaflets to deliver them personally to newspaper offices.

Now the money was all gone, all he could do was hope that his new proposed law would be passed and that just a few more kids like his daughter might have their lives spared if a sufficient deterrent was in place.

> **We have choices even when the most awful suffering comes our way.**

As we shook hands and I drove away I was filled with a sense of deep admiration for this man and his convictions. Yes, you could pick holes in the laws that he was proposing – any law that's going to toughen up on the bad guys is perhaps going to catch a few less culpable people in its net. That's a given.

But I found as I put aside the argument for and against the Three Strikes law, there came a very sober realisation that this man knew what it was to endure great pain, come out the other side, and plant the seeds of that pain in ground which produced a much less bitter result than you might expect.

It wasn't that Mike hated criminals, he just hated the idea that he would spend the rest of his life grieving over his lost daughter and yet fail to serve her memory by making a difference.

So Mike's attitude taught me a great deal and I've told his story often, to illustrate the point that we have choices even when the most awful suffering comes our way. We can consign ourselves to a life of bitterness, regret and hate or we can choose a future in which even the pain becomes a force for good in the lives of others.

In his own way he lived out plenty of truths that can be found in scripture. So that's what I mean about telling real-life stories in a way that we help lift the vision of others.

Schindler's List

Mike's story reminded me so much of the life of Oskar Schindler, whose goodness in saving the lives of several hundred Jews from the Warsaw ghetto during World War 2, was immortalised in print and in the

> **Schindler understands in such a deep way that resources, when used sacrificially, do mean hope and redemption for others.**

movie "Schindler's List".

There's a very powerful scene at the end of the movie, when representatives of the Jewish people he's saved from the Nazis, present him with a ring they've made from gold.

He looks around at these people and realises, perhaps for the first time, the enormity of what it meant to translate resources into saved lives. Schindler gasps as he looks at the Nazi party pin on his own coat. "Two more!" he says on the verge of tears. "I could've saved more!"

He looks desperately at his car and then contemplates other possessions that he might have sold in order to buy the lives of more Jews. At that point Schindler understands in such a deep way that resources, when used sacrificially, do mean hope and redemption for others.

So what's the lesson here? I think it's this: be a gatherer of great stories like that of Oskar Schindler and Mike Reynolds. If you've witnessed this kind of overcoming yourself, it can make for an even more effective story, given that it's touched your own heart through your observations.

Don't be afraid to tell these stories and draw spiritual lessons from them. After all, if people like these can change their lives for good or live sacrificially even without a great spiritual context, how much more can Christians with the power of God learn the value of such living?

If you want to move more into the realm of stories about how faith in God and following Christ's example can help people lead better lives, these stories are everywhere. Here are a few more of the vignettes adapted from segments I wrote for the "Scrubcutter" radio series.

The Kid With the Hot Dog Stand

Who's the most inspiring person you've ever met?

For me, it's a guy you've probably never even heard of. His name is David Bussau, and like a lot of successful Kiwis he's now based in Australia.

David was abandoned at a young age, and grew up in a pretty tough orphanage in a place called Masterton. When he was 15, he set up his first business – a hot dog stand outside the local football ground. It went so well, he established five more hot dog outlets. A regular entrepreneur by the time he was 18.

Finding success in the Australian building industry, and making his first million well before age 30, David was always looking for a way to put his Christian faith into action – in a way that would really benefit the needy.

After visiting Asia, and seeing how hard it was for an ordinary poor person to borrow money, David established a system he calls micro-enterprise. That means loans to the poor at very low interest rates – loans to help poverty-stricken people start a small business that can provide for a family.

David Bussau's idea, started with his own money, has taken off like wildfire. It's working, through community groups all over the third world now. More than two million loan recipients so far. A new job created every three minutes.

The thing about David Bussau is that he's so shy and retiring, he can barely string a few sentences together to stand up in public and tell people about what he's done.

What makes me think he's an inspiration?

Well, among other things, experience tells us a beat up kid from the boys' home in Masterton ought not to have turned out so well. Lawyers defending the violent and the thieving cite bad upbringings in court every day of the week. But David Bussau was different. A strong faith, acquired at an early age, was clearly pivotal.

What David Bussau believes and practices has helped him scale mountains and touch lives in a remarkable way.

■■■■■

I've had the privilege of travelling with David Bussau in East Timor, and seeing, at first hand, his genuine compassion for the poor. In my line of work you get to see sacrificial living in all sorts of settings. The life of the Short family of Christchurch made a particular impact on me, as I explained in a radio piece.

Kids From All Over

The line from the song on the radio bashed me round the head as I heard it over and over the other day. "Only kindness matters, only kindness matters."

It got to me, because that day I got my annual newsletter from the Short family in Christchurch. They've just got to be the best living example of kindness I know.

David and Joy Short were childless. They went to Romania looking to adopt two girls. They were shown lots of gorgeous youngsters, but they had a sense they should take on children with serious needs.

At the little out-of-the-way hospital, someone quietly mentioned "the dying room". That turned out to be a dark enclave out the back, where sickly babies who were not expected to live, were literally left, until they expired.

"We'll take one of those", said David and Joy, and ultimately they returned to New Zealand with two Romanian girls, both with major health problems. Hard work and huge amounts of love saw both girls make great strides.

The Shorts then took on a little boy with significant behavioural problems, but three was still not enough. Next came twins from the Pacific Islands, little girls with severe eating disorders The home of this family of seven, some nights resembled a clearing station in a war zone.

The cost to this once reasonably wealthy couple was enormous. They went from owning a debt-free home, cars, boats and toys, to overdraft and net worth of next to nothing. In the winter, on freezing nights, the twin girls who couldn't eat properly, would regularly need to be rushed to the hospital for tearful reinsertion of the nasogastric tubes they'd pulled out in their sleep.

Bit by bit, the five adopted children have been overcoming huge needs, in the hands of two remarkable parents who have gone from prosperity to the breadline, just because they think kindness and a real chance at life matters so much. They believe they've received so much love from their Heavenly Father, they've got to give some back to needy kids.

Made me think, as we filmed their story, there are angels among us.

■■■■■

I'm convinced that there is always a need to encourage people, more and more so in these times of self-focus, self-interest and rampant consumerism, to keep flying the flag for heroic Christianity.

I've used stories like David and Joy's to illustrate Christian faith in action, in our TV series, "Extreme Close Up". The stories had a great reach into the secular viewing audience – example without too much preachiness.

I've long believed in the potential of the visual media to communicate truth in ways that are sometimes quite subtle, and in the next chapter I want to explore some ways you can use Hollywood's themes and images to your advantage.

–5–

Grab the Popcorn

"Play it again, Sam."

–Humphrey Bogart

If there's one thing I've learned after 25 years in television journalism, it's the sheer power of images. When you weave together just the right mix of pictures and sound, you can make some very useful pieces of communication. Many people who want to teach scriptural principles effectively are now taking advantage of the illustrations that Hollywood and other moviemakers provide us with.

I've used movie clips extensively in my teaching over the last few years and I hope by the sharing of a few examples in this chapter I can get you thinking about the creative use of images in your own teaching.

The interesting thing about movies these days is that in their own way, they're trying to answer many of the questions that we try to cover in our preaching anyway. Issues like life after death, ultimate destiny and the subject of good and evil are all being explored by the movie studios.

I was amazed, for example, when I was recently preparing material for a three-part series on heaven and hell, how many movies in recent years have dealt with the afterlife in quite remarkable ways.

Ghost

The 1990 movie "Ghost" is a classic example. It was one of the most successful films of its time, dealing with what happens to us when we die. Starring Patrick Swayze and Demi Moore, the movie's main character (Swayze) lives on as a troubled spirit after he's murdered in the street. Using a woman – a somewhat larger than life medium – Whoopi

> **He becomes aware that there really are good and bad ultimate destinies depending on how you lived your life on earth.**

Goldberg, Swayze tries to make contact with his bewildered partner Demi Moore. Swayze spends much of the movie negotiating the spirit world in which he becomes aware that there really are good and bad ultimate destinies depending on how you lived your life on earth. There are grim scenes in which bad people, after they've died, are carried away wailing by dark spirits that come out of the ground.

In the end the movie presents some very powerful concepts including the notion that there are consequences to the way we live, there are great and not so great destinations after death, someone's in ultimate control of this realm, and as Swayze comments right at the end of the movie, it's the love you had in this life that you carry over into the next.

In effect, "Ghost" in its own unique way, raises and tries to answer many of the questions we as preachers want to address with people. Even showing the last five to seven minutes of the movie is a good way to bridge into scriptural truth about these matters.

Contact

The movie "Contact", starring Jodie Foster, is another film worth considering as a teaching tool. Foster plays the part of an astronomer, who spends much of the movie in a good-natured debate with a theologian played by Matthew McConaughey. Foster's character, Ellie Arraway, seems pretty convinced there's no

> **In the final analysis a relationship with God has a high faith component which relies on deep personal attachment and experience.**

such thing as an Almighty God. She presses the point continuously: "Show me some proof."

The theologian, Palmer Joss, played by McConaughey, is gentle but relentless in his arguments. At one point he asks her "Did you love your father?" Ellie is taken aback by the question – her dad died an untimely death when she was only nine years old. "Yes, I loved him very much," she replies. "Then prove it!" urges the theologian.

> **Sagan, having dismissed God, really hankered for there to be some benevolent oversight of events here on earth.**

Foster doesn't really get the full import of the question: that while there are aspects of God that are testable and provable, in the final analysis, a relationship with God has a high faith component which relies on deep personal attachment and experience. The rich irony of this concept has a major pay-off later in the movie.

The film's central plot revolves around messages being received on earth by an astronomical team headed by Foster. The messages from a galaxy about 26 light years away teach the scientific team on earth how to construct a transport device, which apparently will enable someone to travel to the source of the messages.

Eventually Foster is chosen as the traveller. She embarks on an eye-popping journey and ends up on a stunningly beautiful beach. There she meets her father again and discovers that Earth's destiny is controlled by an intelligence which transcends space and time.

The trouble for Foster is that when she returns, people simply don't believe her. She ends up in front of a Senate committee, which adopts the same skepticism towards her "experience" which she had previously displayed towards any talk of God.

The movie at this point becomes a good teaching device, in that the awe and frustration Foster wrestles with, is a brilliant reflection of what Christians sometimes feel when trying to persuade others of how stunning it is to have a personal relationship with God.

The added poignancy is that the movie came out of a book by the late atheist astronomer Carl Sagan; and in the end, the central thrust of the story seems to be that Sagan, having dismissed God, really hankered for there to be some benevolent oversight of events here on earth. I'm sure when you watch this movie you may well find a host of other ideas to help stimulate discussion.

Fallen

What I find interesting in many modern films, is the discussion that takes place between actors on what are often fairly deep spiritual matters.

In the movie "Fallen", a cop, played by Denzel Washington, is seen doing battle with a demonic force, which is claiming lives in his patch. The demon passes from person to person by touch and Denzel is hard pressed to figure out what's really going on. One night he becomes engrossed in a conversation about God with a fellow cop played by John Goodman.

Their dialogue is a humorous take on spiritual matters, but in it's own way, is quite a telling comment on the kind of questions many people have about the supernatural realm.

"What's the point of life?" Denzel asks John.

"The point of life is that we catch bad guys."

"Yeah, that's what I used to think, but it's not good enough. What are we doing here? Do you know what I'm saying? Why do we even exist – us?"

"Maybe it's God."

"Yeah, could be. I have a hard job believing we're a part of some huge moral experiment – you know, conducted by a greater being than us. I mean, if he's a greater being than we are, why does he care about us? You know, there's five billion of us, we're like ants. Do we care what ants do, from a moral standpoint?"

"Ants? No."

"Right, so .."

"I'm following you, but at the same time, I'm losing you. Are you heading someplace with this."

"That's my point – are we headed some-place? And if we don't figure it out ..."

"Maybe if you figure it out, you die: heart attack, stroke – you figure out what's what, you don't get to hang around any more, you get promoted. Meanwhile, my wife, she says we're put here to do one thing."

> **Right across the visual and music spectrums, you find levels of yearning for relationship, that are a great lightning rod for teaching.**

"One thing? What's that?"

"Well, it's different, it's different for everybody, with her it's lasagna. And you know when your moment comes, you either do the right thing, or the wrong thing, and you never know when your moment's going to come."

I have used this clip quite often, because buried in the discussion between the two cops, is a whole range of the very issues that trouble postmodern people. As surely as the rock band U2 has written entire musical albums full of huge questions about faith and God, right across the visual and music spectrums, you find levels of yearning for relationship, that are a great lightning rod for teaching.

Sister Act

Another movie I use a lot probably sounds a bit lightweight at first. It's the film "Sister Act" starring Whoopi Goldberg. The central plot of the film revolves around Whoopi's character, a Las Vegas nightclub singer who witnesses a murder and enters police witness protection to keep her safe before the murder trial.

Whoopi is placed in a very unlikely setting – a convent in San Francisco where the nuns have little contact with the outside world. Predictably, Whoopi's character, who's given the name Sister Mary Clarence, finds life in the convent way too restrictive. One evening she takes two other nuns out to a bar. Whoopi's companions find it an eye-opening experience, but when the Reverend Mother gets to hear about the excursion, she's furious and tells Whoopi she's grounded and her only

He was so moved by the triumph of good and courage over evil in the movie, he got up and shouted "Praise God!" in the crowded cinema, during the final moments.

recreation will be to sing with the convent choir.

There's a crucial scene as Whoopi joins the choir at their weekly rehearsal. The nuns can't sing to save themselves and when one of the nuns lets it be known that Whoopi's a singer, the sisters urge her to help them. The choir mistress, an aged and grumpy woman, clearly sees the suggestion as a thinly veiled attempt to oust her from her role. She challenges Whoopi to see if she can teach the nuns to sing properly.

What follows is a classic study in being a change agent. Whoopi organises the nuns into soprano, alto and bass positions then harnesses individuals' strengths and weaknesses within the choir to produce a sound so pleasing that the nuns themselves are amazed. What's more, she keeps the elderly choir mistress on side so effectively, the older woman becomes one of her greatest fans.

The outcome is delightful. By teaching the nuns to listen to each other, express real enthusiasm, and to be visionary about their calling, Whoopi manages to get a sound from the choir that is so appealing the church begins to fill up and ultimately the whole neighbourhood is impacted.

The scenes in this movie, which only take about 12 to 15 minutes to watch, provide marvelous teaching on subjects like change, respect, leadership and vision.

I've used this clip in more conferences than I can remember and you can see the light go on in people's eyes almost immediately. Given that we're such a visual generation I think it's a no-brainer. A tool like this movie brings a teaching session before any size group, from a thousand down to a half dozen, into powerful perspective.

The Matrix

One of the more provocative films of recent years – one that's had lots of Christians talking – has been *The Matrix*. The film, with its depiction of the fight to overcome an evil system in which humans are pawns in an "alternative reality" world, draws on classic biblical themes.

> To prevail, a leader must be found who is capable of immediately seeing the Matrix for what it is so as to effectively counter it.

I have to say, I really enjoyed the film. A pastor friend of mine says he was so moved by the triumph of good and courage over evil in the movie, he got up and shouted "Praise God!" in the crowded cinema, during the final moments when the hero "Neo" appears to ascend into heaven, with echoes of the risen Christ.

Some other Christians have said they've disliked the film intensely. If nothing else, it can provoke great conversations – *The Matrix* having been one of the most successful movies of recent years, especially with younger viewers.

Here's how a Christian film reviewer, Michael Elliott in *The Christian Critic* assessed the movie.

"Imagine if the only world you knew was a lie and truth remained devilishly hidden and shielded from view. That is the secret of *The Matrix*. The Wachowski brothers have succeeded in making a heavily stylized and original film which is not only riveting from an entertainment perspective but is also rife with spiritual parallels. In their movie, the world as we know it is but a complex computer pro-gramme (or matrix) designed to blind people from seeing what is really there... kind of like a Star Trek holodeck of global proportions. The devil does much the same thing, using our five senses' perception to deceive us and prevent us from becoming aware of invisible spiritual realities.

Keanu Reeves is "Neo," a computer hacker who just might be the world's savior, referred to simply as "The One." Even his name means "new," which is what a proper savior provides for his followers:

Many films like "The Matrix" can help you show what real cries come from the human heart, for meaning in a troubled world.

a new beginning.

Having been found and "baptized" into the unfamiliar realm of reality by Morpheus (Lawrence Fishburne), who serves as a kind of John the Baptist figure, Neo undergoes extensive training in order to equip himself for the battle ahead, just as Jesus continually worked the scriptures and grew in understanding for thirty years prior to beginning his earthly ministry.

The enemy? A man-made artificial intelligence that decided it should replace man as the dominant species on the planet, just as Lucifer, an angel created by God, desired to usurp the authority and position of his Creator. Hugo Weaving, as a manifestation of this artificial intelligence, is a chillingly eerie adversary to Neo.

Morpheus and his team of disciples seek to reveal the truth to the unsuspecting world, who are hopelessly dependent upon the system they believe is real. To prevail, a leader must be found who is capable of immediately seeing the Matrix for what it is, so as to effectively counter it, just as Jesus Christ had to learn how to see the devil spirit hierarchy behind the workings of the world in order to combat it.

It is interesting that the home base of the "rebels" is called Zion, for that is the biblical name given to the city of David which figuratively refers to the stronghold of God. It is this base that the enemy wishes to infiltrate and which the disciples vow to defend with their life.

Other spiritual examples abound. There is a "Judas" among the rebels who turns against Neo and Morpheus. We learn that there was a different matrix that preceded the one currently running. In the first matrix, life was perfect but ultimately rejected by man, bringing to mind the biblical record of Genesis and the Garden of Eden. The spiritual concepts of self-sacrifice, believing, resurrection, and prophecy are also present.

The visual impact of this film is outstanding. The Wachowski brothers have imagined a world where reality and virtual reality are intertwined. The details of their unique production style are memorable.

Reeves makes the most of the reluctant hero thrust into a world-saving role. Fishburne plays Morpheus as an enigmatic figure who fully believes that in Neo, he has found "The One."

But should you choose to see *The Matrix*, may I suggest you see it with a Christian friend. Challenge each other to find the biblical parallels. There are many more than are mentioned here. As we condition ourselves to see the truth behind the illusion and the spiritual reality behind the physical reality, we strengthen our resolve and our defences against the one who would have us stay ignorant and in bondage to his lies:

"In whom the god of this world hath blinded the minds of them which believe not, lest the light of the glorious gospel of Christ, who is the image of God, should shine unto them." 2 Corinthians 4:4 [KJV]

■ ■ ■ ■ ■

My advice on a movie like this? See it for yourself. You need to be fairly sure about where you'll be going in a talk in which you use a clip from such a movie, but that shouldn't deter you. My own view is that many films like "The Matrix" can help you show what real cries come from the human heart, for meaning in a troubled world.

Television

The same goes for the teaching potential of television. Sure, there's a danger that you can become a couch potato, but after all there's nothing inherently sinister about that box that sits in the corner of your room. In reality, one of its many functions is that it provides a marketplace of ideas, information and more importantly, real stories about people.

Some of the deepest theological questions you'll ever deal with are canvassed, night after night, on shows like *The Simpsons*.

We're also in an age where there's a flood of information becoming available about the stunning creation in which we live, much of which gives valuable insight and information for sharing with people who we're trying to persuade about their Creator. I always keep a couple of blank video cassettes near my VCR. The amazing thing is, some of the programmes that have me racing to push the record button are often what you'd think of as being the least likely material for talks.

But in reality some of the deepest theological questions you'll ever deal with are canvassed, night after night, on shows like *The Simpsons*.

I have to say there was a time when I considered *The Simpsons* to be quite subversive! I have friends who won't let their children watch the programme, out of concern for the values and ideas it contains.

Funniest thing though, as I've watched this programme over the last few years, I've found it one of the most intriguing shows on air. It often has its own quite powerful sense of morality, and every so often, the characters experience their own quite significant "redemption" in the course of the half hour.

And while *The Simpsons* can often be seen to poke fun at religion, especially Christianity, I think that sometimes the barbs are quite skilfully, even accurately delivered, as it exposes hypocrisy and judgmentalism.

There's one episode I've taped and have used a number of times for teaching, in which The Simpsons are all sitting through a pretty boring church service, and find themselves dropping off to sleep and starting to live in their own Bible dream epics.

The last minute and a half of the programme is actually quite profound as the family wakes up and realises that everyone's left the church except them. "It's okay," says Homer, "it's not the end of the world!" But as the church door opens they realise the Apocalypse has come and some of their friends are being raptured.

Marge soberly wonders whether the reason her family is not lifting off the ground is because of their sins. In its own clever way this scene ends up raising more major theological issues in about 90 seconds than many talks I've heard.

Even Bart Has a Soul

Another *Simpsons* episode that's provided me with a rich source of material lately is to do with the concept of hell and the soul. Bart gets into serious trouble in church and as part of his punishment he has to clean out the organ pipes with his friend Milhous.

As they're doing their chore, they get into a debate about whether humans have a soul. Bart declares confidently there's no such thing as a soul, and Milhous, foreseeing a great opportunity says, "If you're not worried about your soul, then why don't you sell it to me?" They do a deal in which Bart writes out a contract and sells Milhous his soul for five dollars.

Throughout the rest of the episode, Bart gets progressively more paranoid about whether he's going to get into major trouble in the afterlife without a soul. He has vivid dreams in which he sees his friends in rowboats, teamed up with their soul, heading across the water for a final journey to heaven. Bart is stuck in his rowboat and goes nowhere because his soul is nowhere to be found.

In the penultimate scene, Bart falls to his knees by his bed and confesses to God that while he might not have been that well behaved lately, he really misses his soul, is tormented by fears about what might have become of it, and begs to get it back.

As I watch episodes like this, I never cease to be amazed how open many programmes are these days to dealing with supernatural issues, in ways which probably tap deeply-held feelings among many people.

What intrigued me was that as I was editing clips together from the programme to get ready for a Sunday night presentation on heaven and hell, my kids were drawn like magnets to my study to look over my shoulder and begged to be allowed to come along to the presentation because of the visual media I was using to teach on this subject.

In the end we packed out the church for three Sunday nights with about four times the normal attendance and you could have heard a pin drop as we took a tour through *The Simpsons*, the movie *Ghost* and a whole range of other material which explored concepts of the afterlife.

–6–

We Need Heroes

"The bold ones continue. They are eyed by the eagles; the lightning plays about them; the hurricane is furious. No matter, they persevere."
—Victor Hugo

"In your struggle against sin, you have not resisted to the point of shedding your blood."
—Hebrews 12:4

In a telling article in *Newsweek*, Jon Meacham, a young journalist confronted some realities about war and character, with wisdom beyond his years. The 27 year old reporter, in a piece entitled "Where have all the causes gone?" admits:

"People my age face a history gap. With no common enemies, it's not clear how we will react when the inevitable crisis comes." [1]

Meacham reflects that at roughly his age, his grandfather had lived through the Depression in the South, enlisted in the Navy and spent four years at war in the Pacific. His father, at that age, had watched the civil rights movement unfold around him and had fought in Vietnam carrying a 12-gauge shotgun in search and destroy missions.

> **"The toughest combat decision I've ever faced was whether to watch CNN or the networks cover the gulf war."**

By way of contrast the writer says, *"The toughest combat decision I've ever faced was whether to watch CNN or the networks cover the gulf war."*

Meacham makes good sense. I am convinced that one of the things our generation most desperately needs is a regular dose of reality. Especially about its good fortune. As I get older I find myself increasingly entranced

We're preaching to audiences, many of whom have never really lived through the calibre of "troubles" which shaped previous generations.

with stories about war and battle, particularly those of this century. Why? Because for my parents and my grandparents, living through the trials and privations of war, really did shape them.

For all the cute stories we weave into our talks about the frustrations of finding a parking space, or hilarious experiences with the internet, I believe it's just as important to bring the kind of perspective that comes with stories of real struggle, and the overcoming of odds.

I know there'll be some who will disagree with me, but I think we're preaching to audiences, many of whom have never really lived through the calibre of "troubles" which shaped previous generations. Here's Jon Meacham's take on the deal:

"The problem is not our willingness to be moved by events, or causes. The dangerous thing is that without epic scope, every news story becomes a "crisis" and "heroes" come cheap. The cumulative effect of [the media's] confected moments – and the media's appetite for instant drama never helps – is to trivialise just about everything."

Triumph in Hard Times

After nearly 28 years in the media, I have huge sympathy for the point Meacham makes. As I write this chapter, it's just the day after the attack on the World Trade Centre and the Pentagon. When so many stories I've seen, read and indeed written in my career, have contained words like "drama", "shock" and "terrifying", what words do you have left, to describe events such as those which shook the world on September 11th, 2001?

And with which words do you pay tribute to *real* courage.

It's not that you want to try and glorify war in your presentations but I find increasingly these days, I'm turning to the stories about how people made it through when everything was on the line, such as during the early 1940s when Britain was facing the threat of Nazi invasion.

I find it particularly useful to be able to examine the lives of the leaders like Winston Churchill, because of the uncommon heroism of those days, as seen both in Churchill himself and the young men and women who defended their country. It provides stand-out lessons.

I hadn't realised until recently, what a battle Churchill had to persuade other members of his own cabinet to carry on the fight against Germany when so many were urging him to try to appease Hitler by negotiating through the Italian fascist dictator Benito Mussolini. Churchill at the time stood up and said:

"I am convinced that every man of you would rise up and tear me down from my place, if I were for one moment to contemplate parley or surrender. If this long island story of ours is to end at last, let it only end when each one of us lies choking in his own blood upon the ground."

One can only guess what the sheer impact of Churchill's "blood and fire" speeches from those days must have been. He told the young men going into battle, particularly those who were flying in the hopelessly outnumbered fighter squadrons, that the future of Christian civilisation depended on them.

I read recently and marvelled that the average life expectancy of a young fighter pilot in the summer of 1940, during the Battle of Britain, was about two weeks. During those days, there was a high chance that those with whom you ate breakfast would be dead by dinner time.

Why read and tell war stories like these? In the Bible the whole culture of Israel, according to God, was to be built around the concept of remembrance. They were to continually remember through their Feast days and through listening to good teaching, about the faithfulness of God in days gone by, and the stories of how people through faith and perseverance won the prize.

Indeed, even in the New Testament, Hebrews 11 urges us to run our race with patience, based largely on recalling how faith applied, wins the prize.

There's something about the celebration of courage. One of the most inspiring and memorable talks I ever heard from a Christian preacher, was all about the guts, self-sacrifice and leadership of Ernest Shackleton during his ill fated voyage to the Antarctic. How he selected, protected and then saved his men from death, presented not just an astonishing parallel to the process of serving Christ – it also woke up the comfortable yuppie audience who heard the talk, to some great truths about stickability!

Here's how I've used some of the stories about faith and heroism, which have inspired me in recent years, as material for the radio series. Perhaps they'll help you too!

The Columbine Girl

Does having a faith in something make that much of a difference? Perhaps you only really get to answer that question when the chips are down, and you have to lean hard on what it is you believe. Darrell Scott of Colorado, is a case in point. I heard him tell some of his story recently.

Darrell's daughter Rachel was the last teenager killed by Eric Harris and Dylan Klebold on their murderous rampage through Columbine High School in April 1999.

Rachel was taunted by the youths about her Christian faith, then shot dead. Rachel's dad Darrell was as devastated by his daughter's death as any other parent, but when he began to discover what a powerful impact Rachel's life and values were having even after she'd gone, he went on the road, talking to high school kids all over North America, trying to influence youngsters away from violence.

> You can either look at your circumstances he says, or you can see through them, to where you really want to go.

Darrell's seen great results: one tearful youth who heard him, owned up to his own plans to instigate mayhem at his school and turned his life around. Darrell's also had the chance to tell the nation's leaders about his faith and convictions. On May 29th, 1999, he spoke compelling words to congressmen and women.

"Since the dawn of creation there has been both good and evil in the hearts of men and women. We all contain the seeds of kindness, or the seeds of violence. The death of my wonderful daughter, Rachel Joy Scott and the deaths of that heroic teacher and the other eleven children who died must not be in vain. Their blood cries out for answers."

Darrell Scott credits his own and his family's faith with providing the strength for a big task, and he tells his audiences there's a critical attitude involved. You can either look at your circumstances he says, or you can see through them, to where you really want to go.

A "look atter" or "a see througher." Perhaps that's the difference faith really makes.

■ ■ ■ ■ ■

Grandad's Bible

Sometimes life serves up the most amazing surprises. A couple of months ago I was called by a charming elderly woman I'd never met – who said she had a gift for me.

In the bloodstained pocket of two khaki uniforms, something more than a book, close to the heart.

It was a Bible she said had belonged to my grandfather, a Bible he'd carried with him to the battlefields of France during the First World War.

"How did you come to get this?" I asked Sylvie when we finally met.

"Well," she said "your grandfather passed this Bible on to my husband Jack in 1939 when he went off to the Second World War."

"Keep it with you all the time", Granddad had told Jack, "it kept me safe through my war, it'll do the same for you."

Sylvie told me that Jack had kept the little blue Bible on him every day as he flew air force missions over Europe. History now records that Jack and his crew were shot up badly by two German fighters one day in 1942.

By some miracle, they now say, the plane made it back to England, and Jack, although seriously injured, kept firing from the rear of the plane, till both German fighters broke off the attack.

Sylvie said Jack had insisted she find me, Ray's grandson, after he'd died, and hand on the Bible for yet another generation.

I felt pretty humbled as she gave me the Bible that had been a symbol of such hope for two men in two ghastly conflicts.

I had a clear sense they'd both felt it was about much more than luck. In the bloodstained pocket of two khaki uniforms, something more than a book, close to the heart.

■■■■■

Experiences like this, in which you are personally exposed to the courage and faith of another, give you the best of both worlds for a speaking illustration: something you know, and something you felt.

–7–

We Need Perspective

"I long to scale the utmost height, through rough the way and hard the fight; my song while climbing shall resound, Lord, lead me on to higher ground."

–Leonard Ravenhill

"For our light and momentary troubles are achieving for us an eternal glory that far outweighs them all."

–2 Corinthians 4:17

What else do good stories give us? They give us perspective. I'm constantly telling my kids stories about other youngsters who are worse off than they are.

Emotional manipulation? Perhaps, at times, I'd have to concede my dinner table tales about the orphans of Sierra Leone are somewhat self-serving, but nonetheless, there's nothing like a decent dose of someone else's reality to make you realise the level of good fortune we in the modern West can enjoy.

I strongly recommend that you become a collector of useful statistics, which can underscore this contention. Here's a list of facts from the World Health Organisation, which spun off the wire services one day while I was working in a newsroom.

- More than two billion people are sick in the world at any one time.
- Infectious diseases and parasites kill more than 16 million people a year.
- Twenty million women undergo unsafe abortions each year, and 70,000 die as a result.

> **There's nothing like a decent dose of someone else's reality to make you realise the level of good fortune we in the modern West can enjoy.**

Just at the point when I'm about to throw myself a pity party, along comes a lesson which has me scurrying first to count my blessings.

- More than seven thousand adults die each day from TB.
- Seven hundred million people suffer from some sort of mental illness such as neurotic disorders and manic depression
- Diarrhea kills about three million children a year. [1]

And they didn't even cover hunger!

Once again, journalism has given me great personal perspective on my own life. It often seems that just at the point when I'm about to throw myself a pity party, along comes a lesson which has me scurrying first to count my blessings, and secondly, to grab my notebook and start writing.

I relate now a few of those stories which have done it for me. Perhaps they'll encourage you to think of those moments when the light went on for you in the realm of personal wake up calls.

The Bread and the Cross

One time in London I met a guy called Dimitri. He's a journalist who lives in Russia.

We were at a conference for Christian reporters and Dimitri told me and some others a story.

He'd befriended a man in a jail in Moscow. I forget what the man's crime was, but in any event, he'd lost everything – even his family had deserted him.

Dimitri told us the conditions in the jail were appalling. The man he was visiting had 44 cellmates, in one cell that only had 15 beds.

The imprisoned man, who came to faith in Christ, was so touched by Dimitri's ongoing friendship – he wanted to say thank you in a tangible way – but he had no possessions in the jail, in which even writing paper and musical instruments were not permitted.

So Dimitri was flabbergasted, when one day, the man in jail gave him an elaborate crucifix, that looked like it had been crafted from the finest porcelain. How? Asked Dimitri.

What are you doing with all of the resources at your disposal?

The man had saved a portion of each day's bread ration for more than a month. He used the bread to mould a cross, complete with a figure of Jesus on it.

Then he burned the rubber soles of his shoes to make charcoal for one colour, dregs from his tea to colour the body of Christ, and precious drops from his stomach ulcer medicine produced a vivid green. The result was a stunning work of art.

"For you, my friend," the jailed man had said, handing over the creation. When Dimitri held up the cross in the conference, we shook our heads in amazement, then nodded as he asked all of us:

"In the light of the inventiveness of a man who had nothing,what are you doing with all of the resources at your disposal?"

Not a bad question, I thought. What am I doing with what I've got?

■ ■ ■ ■ ■

The Gypsy

I met him in a little town called Berane in the breakaway Yugoslav republic of Montenegro.

A man with a hunted look on his face. He was what we'd call a gypsy – the Europeans call them Romas.

This Roma looked like he'd been on the run for a long time. The man and his eight family members had recently moved into a cabin in a refugee camp beside the river in Berane – a camp administered by an aid agency. He and his family had been chased out of Kosovo and they'd lived out in

The one thing my family and I need most desperately need... is a reality check.

the open for a couple of weeks under trees in sub zero temperatures. Kids and grand-parents, a mum and dad and a little baby.

Their real problem now was that they had no home to go back to. Romas aren't friends with either side in the complex web that is Balkans politics.

Through an interpreter I was able to discern that this 15 thousand dollar cabin about the size of a New Zealand garage was the smartest thing they'd ever lived in.

"So what dreams do you have for your future?" I asked.

The father thought for a moment. "I can only have one dream at a time," he said eventually. "My one dream for right now is for me and my family to stay safe for a bit longer. That's all."

It occurred to me right at that moment that the one thing my family and I need most desperately need is a reality check.

What we would call a "need" in our lives deserves to be regularly measured against the experiences of a man like that.

Telling Stories on Yourself

The art of choosing stories about yourself, and those things you've learned from, is finding those moments that have a strong sense of universal application – stuff that anyone could identify with.

Clever comedians are great at this kind of thing. They often manage to zero in on those things we all wonder about but can never quite articulate.

People experience "truth" and information with their emotions, before the stuff gets to their intellect.

What I reckon is important for the preacher/story teller is the moment of self-discovery. This can be a springboard into all manner of truths. As someone wise remarked to me recently: a great sermon should not only answer the question: what do want them to know, and what do you want them to do; you should also be able to answer this question with confidence: what do you want them to feel?

People experience "truth" and information with their emotions, before the stuff gets to their intellect: that's just a fact of life. Think about a very moving piece of music that has great meaning for you. The sound of it will have a far more profound effect on your heart than your mind.

Here are some more stories involving "self-discovery".

Privileges

A privilege I don't really deserve, but do enjoy as an employee of my company, is membership of the airline lounges at domestic airports. The parking deal is the best thing – you drop your car right outside the terminal. They hand you your keys and the bill with a smile as you arrive back.

We were getting nowhere and the righteous consumer in me was getting cross.

One Sunday morning I got back to Auckland airport from a business trip. I felt pretty mellow. Weather was stunning. The priority baggage deal worked a treat. And the rest of my day was clear.

But my sense of well being didn't last for long. The valet parking counter was closed and there was no one in sight. I could see my car a long way off, parked in the secure area, behind a locked gate.

There were long lines at every other counter, and with my exasperation rising, I went upstairs to the executive lounge and complained. The lounge attendant was great. She tried several numbers, in vain, then accompanied me back downstairs and began rifling through drawers at the parking counter.

We were getting nowhere and the righteous consumer in me was getting cross. Where, for crying out loud, was the person who was supposed to be running this desk? I pay good money for this service; well, not exactly me,

I had become something I once swore I never wanted to be – an arrogant yuppie consumer.

but hey, someone's paying and well, the parking guy or woman ought to be here. The point of it all is that it's supposed to be extremely efficient.

With the tone of a long suffering martyr I told the lounge attendant trying to help me that I guessed I'd just go up to the executive lounge and wait. Which I did. It's nice up there. Got some delicious breakfast, read the paper, and mentally drafted the letter demanding the return of my 36-dollar parking fee, at the very least!

About half an hour later the lounge attendant found me, apologised profusely for the delay, and told me the valet parking person had, at last arrived. Down I went, and in the distance I saw her. The parking woman, that is. Remembered her from a couple of previous occasions. I think I'd seen the nametag once. She was called Sally, I started to remember.

She had one of those faces which looked like it had done a lot of living in just a few years. A face that gave you the sense of someone who's probably raising a bunch of kids in less than ideal circumstances, on whatever huge salary someone like Sally would earn.

She was clearly flustered when I got downstairs, sorting out a lot of stuff, but as I approached the desk, she just tried to act as though things were pretty normal as she gave me my keys and the bill. I felt obliged to tell her I got in 45 minutes ago. Sally said "I'm so sorry, I didn't make it on time today."

I climbed into my car, which by now was right outside and as I drove away I felt a huge vice of conviction around my heart, as I realised several things all at once.

First off, I was a person with power – a senior employee of a major corporate customer of an airline, which probably valued my business, and would very likely give me back my $36 in a heartbeat. Secondly, my complaint would be bad news for Sally. She'd at least face a stern reprimand, at worst, dismissal. Thirdly, I realised was that it was the first day of daylight saving, and there were probably hundreds of people who'd got their times mixed up.

And finally I became aware of this: that without even thinking about it, I had become something I once swore I never wanted to be – an arrogant yuppie consumer.

I think you know what I mean, and I bet that, like me, you've been in on those conversations where you proudly tell your friends [often your Christian ones] how you sorted out some hapless individual who gave you bad service. Or how you stood up for your rights and gave someone a piece of your mind, or how you beat down that street vendor on your latest little overseas sojourn, and paid way below the going rate for your exotic momento.

How "right" and righteous we can be! How easily we buy into the world's value systems. In the process, I realised that the very areas in which I am supposed to be distinctive – in showing mercy and extravagant love and a Christlike nature – are often so far from my mind that it shocks me. The one consolation I have is that I wasn't wearing one of those "What Would Jesus Do?" bracelets. I think I'd have had to hang my head in shame.

The airline won't be hearing from me. That day I really felt it was time, metaphorically speaking, that I had a heart transplant.

■■■■■

Stories in which you discover something about yourself obviously need to be chosen with some care – there is such a thing as too much self-disclosure! My other advice is to keep such stories brief.

If you have stories about your experiences, which do allow you to follow my old boss's brief to "take me somewhere I've never been before," you have potentially great teaching tools.

Ricky's Last Night

Every now and then, in the course of my job as a journalist, I got to go some mind-blowing places. It's in such places you find some things are a

It was all supposed to be straightforward, a jab, and a swift death.

whole lot simpler in theory than in practice.

Take the death penalty for example – never thought a lot about it till I had to go and report on an execution. It was taking place at a jail in Arkansas – that's Bill Clinton territory.

They were going to put to death a guy called Ricky Ray Rector. Eleven years earlier Ricky had shot and killed a policeman in a botched robbery, after which Ricky put the gun to his own head and shot away part of his brain in a suicide attempt.

Although brain damaged Ricky had, they said, embraced the Christian faith in jail and had by all accounts become a model inmate. But he had finally run out of appeals and he was to die by lethal injection.

I guess that up till this point in my life, you could say I had been rather ambivalent about the notion of the death penalty. The idea of hanging and the electric chair were pretty unpalatable to me, but I suppose, if I felt anything I could identify, it would have been "Hey that lethal injection deal sounds pretty quick and painless."

At about 8.30, with half an hour to go before the execution, two of the reporters in our group got the right to go into the viewing room next to the execution chamber. It was all decided by the toss of a coin, and the woman reporter who won the last toss, actually leaped a little in the air with excitement, then flushed a bit with embarrassment at her glee.

It was all supposed to be straightforward: a jab, and a swift death. But the news that came back was grim. They couldn't find a vein in Ricky's arm.

In the end, it took the executioners nearly 50 minutes to end the man's life. It was all quiet in the media room by the time the final announcement came through. The prison PR man in his heavy Southern drawl told us that

There has to be a place, somewhere in our system, for qualities like mercy.

Ricky's last words before he died had been "I got baptised and saved."

To take nothing away from the awful loss

suffered originally by the family of the policeman shot by Ricky, I thought to myself, there's nothing clean about taking a life, whether it's at the hands of a robber, or a state approved executioner.

So how do you handle the crime of murder? It's very tough: I think I'd find forgiveness hard to muster if Ricky's victim had been my dad, I just felt after my night at that jail, that there has to be a place, somewhere in our system, for qualities like mercy. It was a pretty important time for personal reflection.

■■■■■

I guess as a journalist you do get to go some places, like jails where there are executions, places where most people never go – or want to go for that matter.

You don't have to physically be there however, to construct a talk or an idea about a subject. Being well read will give you tons of material.

In the next chapter, I'll talk about turning things you read and observe into messages.

–8–

Collecting Stories From Everywhere

"The gospel is not so much heard as it is overheard."
–Sören Kierkegaard

One of the huge advantages of living in the "information age" is fairly self-evident. Stories are everywhere. In print, on television, on the radio, on the internet. If you're a communicator, be a relentless collector of stories from any publication you can find.

On every overseas trip I make, I amass a huge collection of clippings and torn out articles and weird ads.

Some of the strangest and most useful material is buried away in the back of those giveaway magazines on airplanes. Here's another couple of those radio talks I concocted from such articles.

Marathon Phantoms

Like ghosts who run, there are phantoms who haunt every marathon, disappearing early in the race, then mysteriously materialising at the finish line.

In short, they've cheated. While honest runners rely on their feet to cover the twenty-six miles, these athletes resort to alternative forms of transport, such as bikes, buses, cabs, even subways.

A New Yorker called Fred Lorz is the first known marathon phantom. At the 1904 Olympics he was stripped of his gold medal after admitting he'd hitched a ride in a car for nearly half the race.

These athletes resort to alternative forms of transport, such as bikes, buses, cabs, even subways.

People want to get the T-shirt or the Certificate so badly, they're prepared to go to astonishing lengths.

Does it happen often these days?

Well, yes!

A few years back, an astounding ten of the top 100 finishers in the San Francisco marathon were disqualified. In 1997 the LA Marathon disqualified the women's division winner for taking a shortcut through several gas stations. One guy tried hiding in a portable toilet near the finish line, in yet another race, ready to pop out at the appropriate time.

Why do they do it? Cheat, that is?

Well, fame without pain is the best guess. Success, by way of a few short-cuts. Commentators have suggested people want to get the T-shirt or the Certificate so badly, they're prepared to go to astonishing lengths.[1]

Anyone's who competed in a serious sport knows there are no shortcuts to honest success. Hard work must become a habit. It's the same with building character.

We're in a culture and a time where many of the messages our kids receive, would seek to persuade them that image equals value.

If we want to build character in our kids, we'd better sow in the worth of honest toil early in their lives, and teach them that victories won by lying and cheating are pretty hollow.

■■■■■

The consumer society we're a part of, gives me a near constant series of subjects to speak on. A while ago I read something about compulsive shoppers. This one woman was describing how she tried to control her urge to spend, by putting her credit card in a huge block of ice in the freezer. "It worked for a while," she said, " but then I started to get those urges again. I seemed to be spending my whole life with a wet handbag!"

The plethora of advertising which assails us, throws up opportunities to part us from our hard earned money at every turn. I'm fascinated to read about the obsession we have with owning "stuff", so much of which is ultimately pretty useless. Exploring the sales pitches, and what they tell us about the human condition, is, I've found, a useful bridge into teaching about covetousness and other aspects of our fallen nature. Here's a piece I wrote a couple of years ago.

Safetyman

I have to confess, I'm a bit of a sucker for those wacky sections of airline magazines, which offer toys for grown-ups.

Stuff like a remote that'll find all those lost remotes for the TV and video. A nose hair trimmer, computer software that will write you a love letter. That kind of thing.

There are lepers in your own neighbourhood. They're called the lonely.

The one that really caught my eye on an overseas trip a few years back was an ad for an inflatable companion, for security purposes, you understand!

The full colour ad was for a blowup guy called SAFETYMAN. Now this fellow, when inflated, gives people the impression you have with you a six foot two suntanned male, dressed to your own taste, with air brushed facial features, button on legs optional – but not included in the base price.

Sit Safetyman in the passenger's seat of your car, put him up next to the window of your house, and you'll feel more secure.

Made me quite sad when I read it. Especially after I thought I saw a Safetyman up at the barred window of a tiny apartment one evening in California.

Have we reached the point in sophisticated western society, where the only way some unfortunate soul can feel really safe, is by creating the illusion of strong companionship?

Mother Teresa said, "To those of you who think you should come to India to help my mission, look around you where you are."

"There are lepers in your own neighbourhood. They're called the lonely."

"Go help them," she said, "and you'll be doing a work every bit as enduring as those sisters on the streets of Calcutta."

I had to agree. Safetyman has nothing on a live friend!

Today's Marketplace

> **Jesus effectively picked up the Jerusalem Times of his day, and addressed people through the issues of the moment.**

Every now and then I find myself at a Christian conference listening to a well-meaning guest speaker, who insists he only reads the Bible, because what's in today's newspapers and magazines is way too depressing and he wants to stay "close to God."

I understand the sentiment, but it doesn't work for me. I really want to know what is the heartbeat of today's seekers, and what they struggle with in their world.

It occurs to me that Jesus effectively picked up the Jerusalem Times of his day, and addressed people through the issues of the moment.

"Those eighteen who died when the tower in Siloam fell on them – do you think they were more guilty than all the others living in Jerusalem? I tell you, no! But unless you repent, you too will all perish."

–Luke 13:4

From the pages of today's newspapers – even in the letters to the editor – you are confronted by all manner of material that is rich in potential for exposing the human heart to God's truths.

Here's a letter from my hometown newspaper I spotted just the other day.

It's hard being treated as a leper.

"I love this child with all my being and I would give anything for her to be healthy like your child."

I wonder if many of you out there in "everyday land" have any concept of what it's like to love and live with a brain-injured child? Maybe it's one of those things that you just like to push to the back of your mind, because it happens to other people, thank God, and not to you.

We have a very much loved and cherished daughter who cannot walk very well, she cannot talk very well and a symptom of her condition is that she has regular seizures. She loves to be out and about, she loves shopping and going to the movies like all girls do, because after all she is just a regular kid in so many ways.

So, dear public, there is nothing whatsoever to be scared of, if you happen to witness my daughter having a seizure, or for that matter, any one of the hundreds of people in Auckland who have seizures. It's not catching. You don't have to be embarrassed and look away, pretending you can't see us.

For the reality is that I as a parent am upset and flustered, but to have you treat me as a leper only makes it worse. In fact, a kind word and a helping hand with a now-unconscious child, would really make my day. I love this child with all my being and I would give anything for her to be healthy like your child.

Perhaps you would rather we just stayed home so we didn't remind you that brain injury can happen in the twinkling of an eye – even to you, or one of yours.

Want to stay true to scripture and be relevant at the same time? How many lessons do you think are wrapped up in a letter like that?

How about a fresh take on the Good Samaritan, how about mercy rejoicing against judgement?

People who can move from being grumpy to grateful, will do themselves a huge favour.

How about this:

"The race is not to the swift, or the battle to the strong, nor does food come to the wise, or wealth to the brilliant, or favour to the learned; but time and chance happen to them all."

–Ecclesiastes 9:11

Teaching Gratitude

I am always looking for stories which help me to get an audience to express inner gratitude that "things could be worse for me". What I've learned is that people who can move from being grumpy to grateful, will do themselves a huge favour. So I'm constantly searching out tales that describe the incredible trials some people endure in other countries.

In September 1999, when most of the nightly news coverage was focused on events in the Balkans, I stumbled on a story buried in the world news section of *Time*, which gave me one of the most significant lessons on perspective I ever had.

It was a piece entitled "War Wounds", and it was about the awful suffering of people in the West African nation of Sierra Leone.

Here's just a part of the story:

Sierra Leone's eight-year civil war has settled into an uneasy peace. But it has left a cruel legacy. At the height of the country's chaos this spring, rebel soldiers intensified an ugly ritual of amputations, seizing civilians and chopping off limbs. Human rights groups estimate that thousands have been maimed in this fashion. Two of them told their stories to Malcolm Linton.

Issatu Kargbo is 13, one of seven children of farmer Alimany Kargbo, who moved last year to Samuel Town village, about 30 km southeast of Freetown, because of fighting in his home area. The family lives in a shack in the garden of an abandoned house. Last January 13, Issatu was staying with her aunt on the edge of Freetown, waiting to go for a medical checkup, when rebels overran her neighbourhood:

[Issatu takes up the story] "*It was a Wednesday – a very nice day with the sun shining. The rebels came to the house at around four in the afternoon. There were two: a man about the same age as my father*

"They put my hands on the ground and cut them off quickly."

and a child soldier carrying an ax. They weren't armed, apart from the ax, and they were in ordinary clothes. There were about 15 of us. The man picked out six and took us to the rebels' base at Black Tank. I was frightened because I didn't know what was going to happen.

At Black Tank the man called four other rebels to guard us. A lot of rebels were hiding in the bushes and around the houses. They had a big fire going near the verandah of the house. They ambushed the people who came past and pushed them into the fire, pointing with their guns. They made them lie down in the fire. I saw it happen to five people. Three of them died in the fire, and two managed to get up and walk away, but they were badly burned, so maybe they died later – I don't know.

The children with me were crying. I was more frightened than before because I thought they were going to throw me into the fire. The rebels were laughing and making jokes, except for the man who had picked us out. His face was bad, so dark it was blue – you couldn't see any sign of laughter in it. He cut us with the ax one by one. I was number five. The adults were begging, and the children were crying. They put my hands on the ground and cut them off quickly, the left first. I didn't feel anything, or just something like a sting. Everything went dark, and I fell over on the ground. After a while I got up and walked a little way, but then I blacked out again and fell over. I don't know what happened to the other people. I had no idea why they did that to me. It all took less than half an hour.

I walked back to the house. My aunt saw me and started to cry, but one of the rebels told her they would shoot her if she cried. That night I slept in an abandoned house, and the next day I went down to the main road. A rebel saw me waiting there and took me to the Summer Time clinic [a small clinic with a nurse but no doctor]. He gave me a bowl of rice. Then the other rebels came and took away the rice. They said they would kill anyone who said a word about what had happened. I was in the clinic for a few days. Then the Red Cross came and took me to hospital.

I want to go back to school. I haven't been back since this happened. How can I write? I can't do anything except eat and drink water from a cup. Sometimes I follow my father when he cuts wood to sell in the truck park. I used to wash my clothes and cook. But now I can't do those things. I play with my younger sisters, chasing them and wrestling. I still do that.

I have friends here. They don't make jokes about my arms. They feel very sorry for me. Most of my friends are in Freetown. I want to go back there and see my aunt – just to visit, not to stay. There's no-one at her house to take care of me.

[Issatu's father is humble, polite and upset. "Any time she goes somewhere with us, I want to cry because they have destroyed her looks," he says. Issatu went to Handicap International's clinic in Freetown and got a leather strap to help her hold a spoon on the end of her right arm. She smiles as she shows it off]. [2]

■■■■■

I found this story profoundly moving and incredibly useful for a whole variety of reasons. To ask people to reflect on what life was like for them when they were 13 years old, then compare their lot in life to Issatu's, can produce a sense of perspective that really does bring listeners back down to earth. Try to get people to imagine themselves in this kind of setting. Ask them to then express to God the kind of gratitude they ought to feel.

I'll deal with this kind of up to date material in more detail in the next chapter.

–9–

Staying Current

"Do not forsake me, O God, till I declare your power to the next generation."

–Psalm 71:18

Amazing stuff, just by way of quotes from people in the news, is featured in almost soundbite fashion in our daily newspapers, providing rich sources of material you can build on.

Here's an interesting quote attributed recently to rock star Rod Stewart. It's about marriage.

"The vows should be changed," says Rod, "because they've been in existence for 600 years. Back then people used to live till they were only 35. So they only had to be with each other for 12 years, then they would die anyway."

I didn't hear this myself from Rod's own lips, but it's an intriguing sentiment isn't it. Just the kind of argument you could imagine people having in this fast paced era. It intrigues me because I'm often struck by how much importance we instinctively still place on commitment.

Witnesses in court cases still swear before God to tell the truth, presidents still take oaths of office, we even speak of the difference between sworn and non-sworn police officers.

And if we went to a wedding where there was a kind of non-committal attitude to the relationship, I suspect we'd feel uneasy.

"Do you take this woman to be your lawfully wedded wife, do you promise to care for

No matter how many times people's expectations unravel, I think we still value unconditional love pretty highly.

her in sickness and in health as long as you both shall live?"

If the answer was, "Well that kind of depends... or I'll give it a shot... or yes, but only on my terms", I reckon we'd find that less than satisfactory. No matter how many times people's expectations unravel, I think we still value unconditional love pretty highly.

Just because the dreams don't always come true, there's no reason to lower the bar on commitment. When we at least strive for the happily ever after, everyone wins.

Out of the Mouths...

"I can't escape this enormous sense I have, of a relentless corrosion of the soul."

Sometimes you find telling observations about important issues written up by secular journalists in a way that helps bring issues that concern Christians into sharp focus.

I'll never forget an article by a young woman journalist I was browsing on another plane ride somewhere. What annoys me greatly is that I've since lost the article! Anyway, her words were incredibly memorable, as she confronted the potential cost of her own promiscuity.

Writing about the care young people have to take these days, to demand the truth from potential sexual partners, in an age of HIV-AIDS, she says, at the end of the truth-telling and the truth-evading "I can't escape this enormous sense I have, of a relentless corrosion of the soul."

What They're Saying Out There

A clipping I did retain, and have used quite often, in urging teachers to stay in touch with what some young people think, is likewise, very sad, but telling.

Again it's by a young woman, writing about relationships. Here's what she wrote.
I know two people who are getting married this weekend. This means I

know two people who'll be getting divorced in a few years.

Is this liberation or the upshot of mad expectation?

It's sad, but there it is. Another beautiful love experience booked to end in a wailing heap, mourned by husband and wife until they pull themselves together and pick up someone new at the pub.

We're desperate for passion on the one hand and desperately cynical on the other. We want the best, expect the worst, and get it.

The punch line in the article was grim.

At some point you start finding yourself at parties where you walk into the kitchen and realise you've slept with everyone in it. Is this liberation or the upshot of mad expectation? [1]

I have to say, when I read that article, it filled me with sadness. To think: that's the most some people ever look forward to in the realm of relationships. Rich pickings for a communicator wanting to examine social trends and attitudes.

Many secular writers make quite penetrating observations on life that we would do well to study.

One New Zealand newspaper columnist with a sharp eye for irony, is Rosemary McLeod.

In a powerful article, written not from a Christian perspective, but from sheer human concern, she gives readers her take on the abortion statistics.

Strange isn't it, how the most obvious things don't turn out the way we expect? The mothers of this generation of teenage daughters would have expected feminist soulmates. Instead, what have we got?

In the face of totally convincing evidence that smoking will end up killing you and big advertising campaigns to drive the same message home – they smoke.

In these contemporary girlie magazines, a total absence of advice on how to pursue a serious life committed to human values.

Having been brought up to despise the tyranny of consumerist fashion and conformist body image pressure – they're anorexic and bulimic. Taught to believe in their own unique, intrinsic beauty, they're covered in wacko tattoos and piercings.

Take a look at the magazines they like to read: lead articles cover articles formerly the preserve of pornography. How to give good oral sex. Infallible ways to multiple orgasms. How to masturbate efficiently.

You'll note, in these contemporary girlie magazines, a total absence of advice on how to pursue a serious life committed to human values. With free access to contraception, handed out by non-judgmental professionals, they're getting pregnant in unprecedented numbers. And with abortion available virtually on demand, they're aborting babies as casually as they pierce their belly buttons.

We abandoned the idea of sexual morality, of natural consequences, of sex as part of a committed relationship, or children as part of families. It was the bright idea of people of my generation to sell sex as a theme park, and promiscuity as groovy.

Relationships? Why bother, we said. Men are too hopeless. They're from Mars. We're from Venus.

And now our daughters, still children themselves, are killing our granddaughters. And we're suddenly squeamish. [2]

McLeod drew some criticism for her article. But it occurred to me as I read it, that many of the issues we think as Christians we stand alone on, we don't at all.

Regular secular journalists watch the same trends and are prepared to tell it like it is. Being armed with these viewpoints is often a useful way to hold up a mirror to our society for our listeners.

Beware the Marshmallows

Being aware of useful bits of social research is another great way to illustrate a wide variety of talk subjects.

In 1997, John Ortberg of Willow Creek was delivering a series about developing good attitudes. In one talk, about having an attitude of commitment, he cites research about maintaining self-discipline in the face of temptation.[3]

Kids who delayed grabbing the sweet at age four grew up more socially competent, more confident and were better decision-makers.

John refers to a classic experiment involving kids and sweets.

They sat four-year-olds down at a table and confronted them with a delicious looking piece of marshmallow. The kids were told they could eat, but there'd be benefits if they waited a bit. The idea was to test which kids could delay their gratification.

Researchers wrote up the results, dividing them into what might be called the "grab the marshmallow right now" group and the ones who waited a bit.

They then tracked the children for 25 years. The results were amazing. Those kids who delayed grabbing the sweet at age four grew up more socially competent, more confident and were better decision-makers. They had higher self-esteem, fewer anger problems and were more able to persist than the "grab the marshmallow now" children.

They even became better students. Sadly, those who were less able to resist at age four had more relational problems later and were more likely to end up in jail.

Ortberg had managed to get hold of a clip of news footage from several years ago, which showed kids actually taking part in the marshmallow experiments. It was a highly successful way, at the outset, of drawing in his audience.

Charting the Trends

Being an observer of social trends, then using those observations to create interesting messages, is not hard.

Over a one month period recently, I ripped out interesting columns by three woman journalists in newspapers and magazines, which gave me great material for a talk on character.

Kate Belgrave, the same journalist who wrote about the busted up marriages, also writes challenging remarks about our attitudes to the revelation of faults in the lives of public figures.

It was at a time when a lot of scandal was abroad, involving politicians, high profile sports stars and the like.

The point this columnist was making was that all the outrage was really in the minds of what she called the baby boom generation: those aged between thirty-five and fifty-five.

Gen X, she maintained, is very different in its perceptions of what people do in their private lives. They're much less judgmental, she seemed to be saying.

Here are a couple of quotes:

"By the time we came to adulthood in the early 90's the train had already left. We knew that everyone's private life was a shambles whether they held public office or not.

Most people's parents were divorced or sleeping with each other or coming out of the closet. So I suspect we expect everyone to have a shonky past. We pass very little judgement thereon.

As the Baby Boom generation slowly dies off it'll be better news for those in public life in terms of any skeletons that might come rattling out of their wardrobes.

Don't worry that your past might come up and bite you on the behind one day or that future Prime Ministers will sack you on the grounds of questionable image. You're about to see a generation that truly doesn't give a damn." [4]

My attention was also caught by a column, which appeared in a glossy magazine in the same month, written by a young woman extolling the virtues of swearing.

"It's so common in fact I hardly know anyone who doesn't spout profanity on a regular basis. On the whole we're a generation of guttermouths.

Sure, women might make an occasional half-hearted attempt to cut down on the swearing – that nice-girl stuff can be tricky to ignore – but for the most part we really don't care.

Unless we're in the presence of children. Swear like a trooper, OK but I can't help recoiling when I hear foul language coming out of the mouths of babes." [5]

The third piece was from a writer who was talking about writing out a summary of your life story, for your funeral. Seriously!

She suggests we have such trouble putting it all together for the minister or funeral celebrant when old Auntie Flo dies, we should do it for ourselves – in effect write our own obituary.

Here's what Jill Jamieson writes…

"Now, you're going to feel embarrassed writing nice things about your-self. But why? The accomplishments, the compliments are an important part of what made you the way you are. Give yourself the pleasure of writing the benevolent overview. Then, if modesty is your most important characteristic, rewrite a modified version in the first person.

Now, how do we deal with life's black spots – the time spent in jail after the drink-driving accident, the teenage abortion? Look at it like this: it's your CV for heaven. We need to gloss over some negatives.

Put down the good things that have happened, and the sad things. But you don't have to confess all the bad things you've done. Then you can be content that you've provided an interesting record to be used when the last tributes are paid. [6]

Looking at these three articles, I went on to produce a talk, not so much critical of what the writers were saying, but posing a series of questions about character in an age when, as Kate Belgrave suggests, a lot of Gen-Xers don't "give a damn."

What ought to be the response of a Christian? I asked. Do we have standards on a "sliding scale", or do we hold to some rock solid personal convictions?

Cries From Over the Wall

Every now and then, even a self-confessed atheist is worth quoting.

Alan Duff, one of New Zealand's most acclaimed authors, and an atheist, wrote a fascinating article for a New Zealand newspaper, four days into the new millennium. He's been to church and it had made him think.

He called it, *"Sobering thoughts on turning 50."* [7]

Of course there's a Heaven. I got that line when I was sitting in church in the south Canterbury town of Geraldine on Christmas Day. This voice inside me asked: If they believe it exists, then surely it does?

I thought about if I had one of my children in the cancer ward, dying. What would I say to her or him, what words of comfort would I offer, where would we say that we were going to meet up again? And how would I explain the point of this short existence, what reason to depart so prematurely and in such pain?

> **How would I explain the point of this short existence, what reason to depart so prematurely and in such pain?**

Well, I'd tell my child that she was going to Heaven and that I was coming with her. I'd tell my child that Daddy is right here with her and we're going on this wonderful journey together; it's just that I haven't been given the physical pain to endure along the way, which makes you, my child, even more special, because you're bearing the pain and I'm not sure I could, but I'm coming along.

Your child dying of cancer doesn't need a message from an atheist

When my good Christian friends tell me with a certitude in their eye that they are going to Heaven, who [the hell] am I to say they won't? And what if Heaven is actually a state of mind that you attain in your last moment of conscious awareness? How long, after all, is that last moment, if not infinite?

As an atheist for as long as I can remember God and Heaven have always seemed preposterous to me. And I assumed that since I had arrived at that conclusion objectively, it must be right.

Till I got that thought in a Catholic Church in Geraldine. There was a woman present who sang a beautiful aria, her voice ringing from the rafters above and behind us, and compelling the non-believer to ask himself; so why does she sing so? Is it just to express her voice, or does it express something she believes in?

Why do the churchgoers sing with such feeling? Why do my in-laws have such unshakeable belief? What motivates an 82-year-old priest to keep sermonising with passion?

Your child dying of cancer doesn't need a message from an atheist. Surely the child deserves you, the parent, to give it the best possible place even better than the world she is permanently leaving?

And maybe you, the parent, do get to experience a kind of Heaven yourself in that journey you accompany your child on.

"Which is more than a non-believer deserves, isn't it?"

Now, I reckon there's enough material in that article to keep a preacher going for weeks!

Even if many of the tenets of this man's atheism remain intact after such a deep time of reflection, I think articles like this provide storytellers with a rich vein of material with which to explore the psyche of the kind of person who cries out from behind the wall of his castle, "I want to understand this thing called faith!"

The Search For the Spiritual

Pick up just about any newspaper these days and you'll find the subject of faith and searching for truth, dealt with most candidly.

Here's author Catherine Whitney on "The Forum" page of USA Today in June, 1999, as she speaks about having abandoned her faith, then found herself on a new quest for meaning in life.

> **"I was struck with a tremendous longing for the faith I had once embraced so completely."**

My father's death... jolted all of my senses and tore deeply at the packed earth I had placed against the roots of my buried faith.

As I stood with my family in the cemetery and watched my father's coffin lower into a freshly dug hole in the earth, I was struck with a tremendous longing for the faith I had once embraced so completely, the hard-core faith of my youth when I could have said with certainty, "I'll see my father again."

I wanted to believe that he wouldn't just disappear into the wet, cold earth and be forever gone. But I had lost that child's knack of believing. Now, as a grown-up, I didn't know where to begin.

Ever since that moment, standing before my father's grave, I've been on a journey, searching for my faith on the winding path back to belief. I'm not alone. All around me, I am joined on my quest for a renewal of faith by an entire generation of seekers. It may have seemed easy to abandon religion while we were in our twenties, but it has become increasingly clear that we aren't willing to face our later years without it.[8]

Such articles help teach us timeless truths, including the powerful way in which tragedy brings people relentlessly back to God.

–10–

Make 'em Laugh

"Don't take life too seriously. You'll never get out alive."

–Bugs Bunny

Someone once said something really smart about laughter: If people are laughing, their defences are down. As we approach our job as communicators, the ability to create genuine mirth and humour in an audience, is a gift we ought to cultivate.

Too often, we are delivering a "yes" message with a "no" face, forgetting that great principle of scripture that a merry heart does us good, just like a powerful medicine.

The best sort of humour is that which comes out quite naturally.

I advise speakers in my training seminars, to figure what "style" of humour they have [if any!] and use that style to their advantage. In other words, the best sort of humour is that which comes out quite naturally. Get some advice on this, from those who know you and love you. A smile and some cleverly targeted stories can work wonders.

I often draw on things that have made me laugh during my years of reporting. In journalism we used to have a phrase called "The Silly Season". That was the time of the year, usually around Christmas where I come from, during which time, normal news sources shut down for the holidays, and reporters, with not much to write about, start making up stuff, and passing it off to the readers and listeners as real news.

Here's a classic example from the wires a couple of years ago:

The Killer Hippo

A Thai newspaper reports that a vegetarian hippopotamus has swallowed a circus dwarf in a freak accident in the north of the country.

The one thousand spectators continued to applaud wildly until they realised there had been a tragic mistake.

The paper says the circus dwarf died when he bounced sideways from a trampoline and was swallowed by a yawning hippopotamus which was waiting to appear in the next act.

Vets say the hippo had a gag reflex, which automatically caused her to swallow.

They say in mitigation that the animal was a vegetarian who had not previously digested a circus performer.

The paper says unfortunately the one thousand spectators continued to applaud wildly until they realised there had been a tragic mistake.

Police say the trampoline had been sent for forensic analysis.

Here's the interesting part: one time I told this story, a policeman who'd been listening came up to me all concerned because he'd heard the story on the radio, and really believed it was true.

He was kind of mad at me for suggesting that the story might not be accurate! I hope it's not *my* home burglary he gets to investigate next week!

As storytellers, we need to find things which reflect the everyday struggles our listeners are probably experiencing. The battle to lose weight is a classic example. One statistic suggests that of all people who go on diets, only five percent keep weight off in any meaningful way, long term.

Here's a diet guide I picked up – obviously written by someone who has trouble balancing dietary discipline with daily stress.

The Stress Diet

Does stress affect your eating habits? This diet is designed to help you cope with stress that builds up during the day.

Breakfast
One grapefruit
One slice unbuttered wholemeal toast
Large glass of skim milk

Lunch
One cup legumes
One cup steamed spinach
One cup of herb tea
One iced cookie

Afternoon Tea
Rest of the iced cookies
Two litres of Rocky Road Icecream, with nuts, cherries, whipped cream and chocolate sauce.

Dinner
Two loaves garlic bread with cheese
Giant Mexican or Hawaiian pizza
Four cans or one jug of beer
Three chocolate bars

Supper
Entire frozen dessert eaten directly from the freezer

> Things licked from knives or spoons have no calories if you are in the process of making something.

Rules of the Diet

- If you eat something, and no one sees you eat it, it has no calories.
- If you drink diet coke/lemonade with a chocolate bar, the calories in the chocolate bar are cancelled out by the diet drink.
- When you eat with someone else, calories don't count if you don't eat

more than they do.

- Food used for medicinal purposes has no calories, e.g. hot chocolate, brandy, toast and ice cream.
- Movie related foods have no calories, as they are part of the entire entertainment package and not part of one's personal fuel, e.g. marsh-mallows and potato chips.
- Broken cookies have no calories. The process of breaking causes calorie leakage.
- Things licked from knives or spoons have no calories if you are in the process of making something, e.g. peanut butter when making a sandwich, ice cream from a spoon when making a sundae.
- Foods that have the same colour have the same calories, e.g. mushrooms and white chocolate, spinach and kiwifruit icecream.

NOTE: Chocolate is a universal food colour and may be substituted for any other food.

Don't be afraid to seek some loving counsel from time to time, as to whether a given story really worked or not.

When trying to use jokes, you have to be a little careful. Nothing falls as flat as a badly told or ill-timed joke. The way you weave funny stories into your message is something that's worth spending some time on getting right. Once again, don't be afraid to seek some loving counsel from time to time, as to whether a given story really worked or not.

If it's of any help, here's one that usually works for me:

The Perils of E-Mail

As you are receiving e-mail, it's wise to remember how easily this wonderful technology can be misused, sometimes unintentionally, and with serious consequences.

Consider the case of the Illinois man who left the snow-filled streets of Chicago for a vacation in Florida. His wife was on a business trip and was planning to meet him there the next day. When he reached his hotel, the man decided to send his wife a quick e-mail. Unable to find the scrap of paper on which he'd written her e-mail address, he did his best to type it in from memory. Unfortunately, he missed one letter and his note was directed instead to an elderly preacher's wife, whose husband had passed away only the day before. When the grieving widow checked her e-mail, she took one look at the monitor, let out a piercing scream, and fell to the floor in a dead faint. Hearing the scream, her family rushed into the room, and saw this message on the screen.

"Dearest Wife, Just got checked in. Everything prepared for your arrival tomorrow. P.S. Sure is hot down here."

Be a little careful with your timing on this one!

Bloopers

There's a never-ending attraction to stories about human frailty and mistakes. Charlie Chaplin and Buster Keaton proved this in the early silent movies, the "Funniest Home Videos" series in all their permutations, have cashed in big on the tradition, and there are some pure gems around in written form, which are great ice-breakers.

Exam bloopers collected from the writings of college students are a load of fun. Here's a selection I've had floating around in my so-called "Fun File" for several years.

Ancient History

"The inhabitants of ancient Egypt were called mummies. They lived in the Sarah Dessert and traveled by Camelot. The climate of the Sarah is such that the inhabitants have to live elsewhere, so certain areas of the dessert are cultivated by irritation. The Egyptians built the Pyramids in the shape of a huge triangular cube. The Pyramids are a range of mountains between France and Spain.

The Bible is full of interesting caricatures. In the first book of the Bible, Guinesses, Adam and Eve were created from an apple tree. One of their children, Cain, once asked, "Am I my brother's son?" God asked Abraham to sacrifice Isaac on Mount Montezuma. Jacob's son Isaac stole his brother's birth mark.

Pharaoh forced the Hebrew slaves to make bread without straw. Moses led them to the Red Sea, where they made unleavened bread, which is bread without any ingredients. Afterwards, Moses went up on Mount Cyanide, to get the Ten Commandments. David was a Hebrew king, skilled at playing the liar. He fought the Philatelists, a race of people who lived in Biblical times. Solomon, one of David's sons, had 500 wives and 500 porcupines.

History calls people Romans because they never stayed in one place for very long. At Roman banquets, the guests wore garlics in their hair. Julius Caesar extinguished himself on the battlefields of Gual. The ides of March murdered him because they thought he was going to be made king. Nero was a cruel tyrant who would torture his poor subjects by playing the fiddle to them."

More Enlightened Times

"The Renaissance was an age in which more individuals felt the value of their human being. Martin Luther was nailed to the church door at Wittenberg for selling papal indulgences. He died a horrible death, being excommunicated by a bull. It was an age of great inventions and discoveries. Gutenberg invented the Bible. Sir Walter Raleigh is an historical figure because he invented cigarettes. Another important invention was the circulation of blood. Sir Francis Drake circumcised the world with a 100 foot clipper."

Musical Notes

"Bach was the most famous composer in the world, and so was Handel. Handel was half German, half Italian and half English. He was very large. Bach died from 1850 to the present. Beethoven wrote music even though he was deaf. He was so deaf he wrote loud music. He took long walks in the forest even when everyone was calling for him. Beethoven expired in 1827 and later died for this."

Childish Wisdom

Things that kids say are always a great ice-breaker or source of illustration. Here's a selection of kids' tips on love.

"If you want to be loved by someone who isn't already in your family, it doesn't hurt to be beautiful."

On what is the proper age to get married?

"Eighty-four, because at that age you don't have to work any more, and you can spend all your time loving each other in your bedroom." [Judy, age 8]

"Once I'm done with kindergarten, I'm going to find me a wife." [Tom, 5]

On what most people do on a first date?

"On the first date, they just tell each other lies, and that usually gets them interested enough to go for a second date." [Mike, 9]

On when it's OK to kiss someone.

"You should never kiss a girl unless you have enough to buy her a big ring and her own VCR, 'cos she'll want to have videos of the wedding." [Jim, 10]

On the great debate: get married or stay single?

"It's better for girls to be single, but not for boys. Boys need someone to clean up after them." [Lynette, 9]

"It gives me a headache to think about that stuff. I'm just a kid. I don't need that kind of trouble." [Kenny, 7]

On the role of good looks in love.

"If you want to be loved by someone who isn't already in your family, it doesn't hurt to be beautiful." [Jeanne, 8]

"Beauty is skin deep. But how rich you are can last a long time."
[Christine, 9]

Some surefire ways to make a person fall in love with you.

"Tell them that you own a whole bunch of candy stores." [Del, 6]

"Don't do things like have smelly, green sneakers. You might get attention, but attention ain't the same thing as love." [Alonzo, 9]

"One way is to take the girl out to eat. Make sure it's something she likes to eat. French fries usually works for me." [Bart, 9]

On how to make love endure.

"Spend most of your time loving instead of going to work." [Tom, 7]

"Be a good kisser. It might make your wife forget that you never take out the trash." [Randy, 8]

■■■■■

Some of the best humour you will encounter comes from the great contrasts you discover as you look back in time, and compare attitudes now, towards subjects like equality of the sexes, to the way it used to be.

The Way We Were... Or Were We?

Floating around my workplace recently, I found an amazing series of guidelines for young wives, as printed in a 1950's high school home economics textbook.

Minimise all noise. At the time of his arrival, eliminate all noise of the washer, dryer or vacuum.

It tells girls how they ought to behave once they're married, and there is a particular section on preparing the home for "the master of the house" in the evening. It's a classic.

Have dinner ready, Plan ahead, even the

night before, to have a delicious meal ready on time for his return. [This is a way of letting him know that you are thinking about him, and are concerned about his needs. Most men are hungry when they come home and the prospect of a good meal – especially his favourite dish – is part of the warm welcome needed.]

Prepare yourself. Take 15 minutes to rest, so you'll be refreshed when he arrives. Touch up your make up, put a ribbon in your hair, and be fresh looking. He has just been with a lot of work-weary people.

Be a little gay and a little more interesting for him. His boring day may need a lift and one of your duties is to provide it.

Clear away the clutter. Make one last trip through the main part of the house just before your husband arrives. Gather up schoolbooks, toys, paper etc, then run a dustcloth over the tables.

In the cooler months of the year, you should prepare and light a fire for him to unwind by. Your husband will feel he has reached a haven of rest and order, and it will give you a lift too. After all, catering for his comfort will provide you immense personal satisfaction.

Prepare the children. Take a few moments to wash their hands and faces, comb their hair, and if necessary, change their clothes. They are little treasures and he would like to see them playing the part.

Minimise all noise. At the time of his arrival, eliminate all noise of the washer, dryer or vacuum. Try to encourage the children to be quiet. Be happy to see him.

Listen to him. You may have a dozen important things to tell him, but the moment of his arrival is not the time. Let him talk first. Remember, his topics of conversation are more important than yours.

Don't ask him about his actions or question his judgement or integrity. Remember, he is the master of the house, and as such, will always exercise his will with fairness and truthfulness. You have no right to question him. A good wife always knows her place.

I brought out this document and innocently asked Ali whether she thought it might provide quite a sound model for restructuring our home environment. I'm not sure what happened in the next few moments – just that I woke up some time later wearing a piece of garden furniture around my neck, and my head hurt rather a lot.

The Dark Side

Owing to my background in journalism, I developed over the years, what many reporters acquire, and that's a sense of black humour. Not salacious, you understand, just that weird Far Side bent that means you're forever getting into trouble when you preach, because you're bound to offend someone!

The upside is that some people love this stuff, especially stuff that pokes gentle fun at cotton candy sayings.

Things to Remember

Do not walk behind me, for I may not lead. Do not walk ahead of me, for I may not follow. Do not walk beside me, either. Just leave me alone, you are bothering me!

It's always darkest before dawn. So if you're going to steal your neighbour's newspaper, that's the time to do it.

It may be that your sole purpose in life is simply to serve as a warning to others.

If you think nobody cares if you're alive, trying missing a couple of car payments.

Timing has an awful lot to do with the outcome of a rain dance.

Eagles may soar, but weasels don't get sucked into jet engines.

Before you criticise someone, you should walk a mile in their shoes. That way, when you criticise them, you're a mile away and you have their shoes.

You should never say anything to a woman remotely suggests you think she's pregnant, unless you can see an actual baby emerging from her at that moment.

There is a very fine line between "hobby" and "mental illness."

Don't squat with your spurs on.

And Finally... For the Deeply Disturbed

Next time you're having a bad day, recall:

The average cost of rehabilitating a seal after the Exxon Valdez oil spill in Alaska, was $80,000. At a special ceremony, two of the most expensively saved animals were released back into the wild amid cheers and applause from onlookers. A minute later they were both eaten by a killer whale.

In 1992, Frank Perkins of Los Angeles made an attempt on the world flagpole sitting record. Suffering from the flu, he came down eight hours short of the 400 day record, his sponsor had gone bust, his girlfriend had left him, and his electricity had been cut off.

A woman came home to find her husband in the kitchen, shaking frantically with what looked like a wire running from his waist towards the electric kettle. Intending to jolt him away from the deadly current, she whacked him with a handy plank of wood by the back door, breaking his arm in two places. Until that moment, he had been happily listening to his walkman.

Two animal rights protestors were demonstrating at the cruelty of sending pigs to the slaughterhouse in Bonn, Germany. Suddenly the pigs, all two thousand of them, escaped through a broken fence and stampeded, trampling the two hapless protestors to death.

And spare a thought for Iraqi terrorist Kay Rahnajet, who didn't pay enough postage on a letterbomb. It was returned to Kay, who, forgetting it was a bomb, opened it, and blew himself to bits.

[I have absolutely no idea of the source or the veracity of any of the above stories].

–11–

Selecting Your Subjects

"There's one born every minute."
—P.T.Barnum

"Therefore be wise as serpents and harmless as doves."
—Matthew 10:16

Indulge me for just one chapter if you will, and allow me to wear my journalist's hat. I want to suggest to you, that one really important rule in this process of illustration, is this: BE DISCERNING!

If there's anything that really concerns me about some modern-day preaching, it's that we're often way too gullible with the stories we buy into.

I think it springs from a wider issue. At least once a week, I get one of those panicky mass emails from somewhere, which warns me my computer's about to go into meltdown in the next two hours, because of some bug from Guatemala that's infesting the Internet.

Most often, there'll be a correction within half a day or so – "Sorry folks," the embarrassed follow-up email will say – "I got suckered by an urban myth." You know the maddening part? Many of these false alarms come to me from Christian acquaintances.

They're the same people who mass circulate their friends demanding you sign their email petitions because they're reliably informed the US congress is about to pass laws making it illegal to mention God's name in TV sitcoms.

Either that, or it's some astonishing [but usually untraceable] video footage of the face of Jesus appearing in some ice cream that was spilled on the floor of an obscure French monastery. You know the kind of thing!

Urban Myths Galore

I used to get quite excited about all this once upon a time, because you hear this stuff from people you trust who swear blind that it's true. Potential use as talk material? Probably because of my incurable journalistic instincts, the potential for me is quite high! I love the tension and release deal, even if it does end with the realisation that the story turns out to be [usually] a complete fiction.

Several years ago now, we got a call to my newsroom from someone who told a breathless tale about a young couple from Christchurch, New Zealand. The caller said the man and woman had just finished up a great two week vacation in Bali. On the last night of their holiday, the man went out for a drink at a local bar, while his wife packed their suitcases back at the hotel.

An autopsy revealed both his kidneys had been removed! He'd become part of the awful international trade in body parts.

The guy didn't return till nearly 5am. He kind of slumped in the door of their room, and she assumed he'd just drunk too much, so she called a cab to take them to the airport for their flight home. He looked terrible as they boarded the plane – was almost incoherent, in fact. About half way into the return trip, he mumbled that he felt awful and went to the toilet, where he died a short time later.

They apparently rushed his body to the morgue, as soon as the plane touched down, and were horrified to discover two freshly sutured wounds on his lower back. An autopsy revealed both his kidneys had been removed! He'd become part of the awful international trade in body parts.

Try as we might, we could never find the widow. Funny that. Years later someone gave me a warning bulletin that was posted to Air New Zealand pilots, warning them to avoid bars in New Orleans and Houston. Guys were turning up dazed and sore in baths full of ice after a night on the booze, finding themselves hooked up to saline drips, and with a number for the paramedics taped to their chest.

You guessed it – minus a kidney! The airline pilots bulletin even had a Florida hotline you could call for more information. I dialled the number – it was a weary sounding voicemail service. I forget the exact words. The general idea though: you've been conned.

If I now had a dollar for every one of these tall tales I'd been told, I'd be rich enough that I wouldn't need to write this book!

Christians get a reputation – and it's often well deserved, for being really gullible, when it comes to the stories we believe and tell.

The problem with all this? It's most often my wide-eyed Christian friends that tell me these stories. But I think it sometimes goes deeper. We love conspiracy theories! Christians get a reputation – and it's often well deserved, for being really gullible, when it comes to the stories we believe and tell. I think the area of prophecy is a case in point – especially so, back around the turn of the millennium.

A columnist in the New Zealand Herald noted:

"The potential for extraordinary millennium hysteria is in the air. One is already conscious of attempts by various wide boys to play on it.... We must keep ourselves in check. We're not at our best when we panic, particularly when we get apocalyptic on it." [1]

When I was travelling in the US with my family in the early summer of 1999, I took particular note of what was being predicted by widely read Christian commentators, about the approach of the year 2000. Frankly, I was dismayed, and I reflected my concerns in a series of talks I gave in September 1999 – a series called "Y2K... What, me worry?"

Not to say I told you so – but purely to refresh your memory about those times, let me tell you some of what I said, in that series. Perhaps it will help to illustrate the need for caution about story selection.

What... Me, Worry?

I wonder if any of you are starting to share my sneaking suspicion? That we might actually make it past January 1st, 2000, without a global financial meltdown, major power crashes, and the inadvertent launching of hundreds of non-Y2K compliant nuclear missiles?

In case you've just returned from a five year Tibetan retreat, and don't know, the Y2K deal goes like this: a number of years ago when we were programming computers, we took a short cut.

Memory was precious back then, so instead of writing 1999, we wrote 99 instead. As the millennium drew closer, a vital question arose. When 99 rolls over to 00, will the computer chips around the world which are date sensitive, get horribly confused, think we've gone back to the year 1900, and shut down, causing global chaos?

It's clear the problem is real. Experiments have been carried out. In some buildings, electronic clocks were rolled forward, and the systems controlling services like elevators, were confused. The phenomenon was given a name: the Y2K problem. Urgent efforts have been underway to fix it – reconfiguring non-compliant systems, and ensuring all new equipment is bug-free.

When the Y2K issue first got serious publicity, it felt like manna from heaven for two groups: journalists and "commentators" – people who make their living advising the rest of us how we ought to face a given issue, based on their specialist knowledge.

Experts consulted by Britain's Sunday Times newspaper in 1996 said "This is not a prediction – the Y2K bug – it's a certainty. There will be serious disruption in the world's financial services industry. It will be ugly. A millennium – induced market crash will happen in mid 1999."

One of America's most widely quoted Y2K commentators, Gary North, is predicting a massive run on the world's banks. "There will be a bank run like no other, all over the world in 1999. A world – wide panic is now inevitable," says North. Or check out the future as painted by another millennium doom monger, Donald McAlvaney: "The year 2000 represents a cyber nightmare, that could throw our entire high tech civilisation into total chaos and gridlock and it is guaranteed to occur."

Other Y2K commentators have said things like:

"There will be a seven to eight year economic collapse after the year 2000."
"Unprepared families risk hunger, disease and hardship."
"There will be anarchy, great crowds of refugees marching across the country. There will be 70 percent job losses in the industrialised world."

> **Christian commentators appear to be among the most vocal, in raising an enormous chorus of gloom, about the year 2000.**

Danny Hillis, a computer specialist of a somewhat different persuasion, wrote in Newsweek recently, "I believe it [panic over Y2K] is because this story has all the makings of a Great Rumour: convincing detail, cooperative experts and a hint of deeper truth."

The experts [so-called] says Hillis, are always willing to speculate. Perhaps pacemakers have calendar routines? Perhaps elevators will crash? Perhaps, maybe, there's a chance, we can't exclude this or that, and so it builds.

Around the world this has generated a massive book and TV industry, particularly on Christian television in the United States, where two or three times a day there are preachers and commentators talking about the disaster that's about to befall the earth. It is usually tied in with some pretty heavy talk about the judgement of God.

In America, there is now huge business in survival gear, many of the companies run by Christians. They offer a couple of years' supply of canned and dried food, tents, generators, and advice on attack dogs and firearms. One pastor has been giving his congregation instructions on how to trash your own house, so that when marauding gangs come along in the millennium chaos they will think that your house has already been done over!

One prophet of doom has an interesting spin on the coming disaster: although he expects the overthrow of current governments, even civilisations, he advises subscribing to his newsletter which will be delivered, he hopes, until well into the year 2000. So he presumably believes the US

Postal Service will be the one system that will survive the predicted chaos!

The worrying thing for me is this. Christian commentators appear to be among the most vocal, in raising an enormous chorus of gloom, about the year 2000. The predictions I mentioned above, are by no means the most outlandish that have been made.

Secular journalists and authors have already tumbled onto the fact that some of the more dramatic Y2K predictions being touted around churches and Christian conferences, have no basis in fact, and are built upon second hand stories derived from unsubstantiated sources.

Maybe it's time for some reality checks:

1. We already know that the improved systems will work – ones that have been made Y2K compliant. Computers are already coping with bank card expiry dates well into the next century, mortgages that don't mature, as in my case, until the year 2100! They are also coping with the prisoner release dates well into the next century: in other words when these numbers are entered into a computer, the computers don't crash. These systems are supposed to crash in a few months' time, but have already proved that they are coping and are not falling over.

2. Will it all be done in time? One of the great fears was that there would be so many lines of code to change within computers, that banks and other big financial systems with lots of lines of code would not be able to get it done in time. Well in fact, highly efficient new software has now been invented and while there was great concern, banks which started out with 400 million lines of code to alter, now have software that does four million lines in an hour. So it can be done in a matter of days or weeks.

3. As to what Christians "in the know" really think, there was a survey done recently of 100 Christian computer companies. They were asked to rate the likely impact of Y2K on a scale of one to ten. The average was around 2.5 – which they said, was about the equivalent of a severe winter storm, on their rating scale. A long way short of the prediction by the head of a major Christian ministry, that we are headed for "the

greatest social, political and financial crisis mankind has faced, likely to lay low the governments and economies of the whole world."

4. People are understandably worried about hospitals. What is going to happen if all the equipment starts to fail and I'm on a cardiac machine or something that is keeping me alive? In the Western United States tests were performed recently across a network of 34 hospitals, with 40,000 pieces of medical equipment, and they found that only nine machines experienced Y2K problems. All apparently fixable.

5. Is it safe to fly? People are worried about planes falling out of the sky. The Boeing Corporation has done quite a number of checks across all of their fleet and they have concluded that only a very few systems within aircraft use the date function in their computer chips and none of the systems related to in-flight safety.

> **When we start saying definitive things about dates, we lay our message open to ridicule, when what we say doesn't happen.**

6. Will your money be safe? Here in New Zealand the banks have done thousands of tests to see what would happen on January first to individual account balances, automatic payments, and inter–bank transactions. They tell us things worked just fine.

Self-Fulfilling Prophecies

Fears remain, and some of them are perhaps reasonable. What will happen if the Third World banks, for example, are not all compliant?

Trouble is, much of the current concern derives, as I have suggested not from hard data, but from rumour and speculation. No matter how much reassurance is forthcoming, stories of potential disaster, as with many urban myths, take on a life of their own.

The big fear of course in all of this is, that people will panic anyway. If enough people buy the hype, there will be a run on the bank, the shelves will be stripped, and people will behave irrationally. They did a survey in the States recently because someone gave out the advice, "You should all stock up and get enough food for a year."

Well, they found that even if just a few thousand people did that, it would basically strip shelves in every supermarket in the US. So what's all the fuss about anyway? Why have people made a big deal about the year 2000?

The year 2000 is a highly quoted year by modern day predictors of the end of the world. Some believe God is about to bring judgement on the earth over the next few months.

This is not the time or place to explore this viewpoint at length, other than to say the business of predicting Armageddon is fraught with difficulty. Perhaps you've heard of books like "Eighty-eight reasons why the Rapture could be in 1988," and some of the hundreds of other publications which assured us Jesus would be back before the millennium.

Clearly there's validity in bringing a warning to the earth about the Lord's return. There is a lot at stake. But when we start saying definitive things about dates, we lay our message open to ridicule, when what we say doesn't happen. It's not good enough that people make predictions that don't eventuate on the given day, then simply shrug their shoulders and say they must have got it wrong.

> **Of all the people on the earth, we ought to be those filled with a sense of confidence about the future.**

A recent occasion on which people really got egg on their face was in the Gulf war. Did you know that Saddam Hussein was supposed to be the American president by now? In 1990 and 1991 when the war was on, there was substantial airtime given on Christian television to commentators saying that the Arabs were going to beat America and Hussein would be installed in the White House.

Leaving a Better Legacy

Here's my concern about all this stuff. Seems to me, it must have an influence on how seriously the world takes our words. If the new century dawns without the kind of disaster so many have predicted, what does that do to the non-Christian's perception of prophecy?

I would submit that we must leave a better legacy to future generations of believers. We have so much good we can do and say. The real power of the Christian message has always been in this: its ability to change lives in the here and now through authentic relationship with Christ, and through the process of discipleship, led by Christian example and love.

My remarks are no in sense intended to criticise those who feel it's right to make some modest plans, in case there's difficulty in January. I simply suggest that of all the people on the earth, we ought to be those filled with a sense of confidence about the future and the one who holds it, rather than being focussed on hoarding food and stashing cash.

One Christian author has suggested the "bug" we ought to be most concerned about is not Y2K but "EWJ" – that is, Eternity Without Jesus. It's a plague on the earth, claiming millions of lives every year.

We know for an absolute certainty that this is, and will be, the most deadly virus facing humankind. If we were half as concerned about this bug as Y2K, we would be doing the world a huge service. [2]

■■■■■

As well as giving a three-part message in my home church, I turned the above remarks into a magazine article. The research for the talks taught me the value of checking sources for the stories we use.

As a journalist who is also a Christian, I make a strong plea to preachers and teachers to only use stories, illustrations and information that we are sure are true.

–12–

Faith in Real Life

"I am only one, but I am one. I cannot do everything,
but I can do something."

–Edward Everett Hale

What I have to say in this chapter may sound blindingly obvious. But it goes like this. We need to remind people that they have a supernatural God. We'll probably give plenty of talks in our lives about how to build better relationships, raise our kids more effectively, and exercise forgiveness, and in many ways these subjects are right at the very heart of our message.

However we often find ourselves talking about these principles as ideals, couched in fairly general terms, and there's nothing like having actual stories of where people have managed to put the broad principles into practice, to help encourage listeners. In my TV series "Extreme Close Up", about faith in real life, one of the things we strove hard to do was find people who, for example, had exercised forgiveness and faith in the face of overwhelming adversity. David Green was a case in point.

On a terrible winter's day in 1995, an Ansett Airlines plane en route from New Zealand's largest city Auckland, to the small provincial centre of Palmerston North, got caught up in some extremely bad weather. To make matters worse, as the crew tried to bring the plane into land they struck a problem with the aircraft's landing gear.

Before anybody really appreciated how serious the problem was, the plane had crashed. The Dash-8 aircraft broke into several pieces on the rain-swept hillside. Three people, including a flight attendant, died at the scene and others who had suffered a range of injuries from minor to serious were airlifted to a nearby hospital. Among those who had been

David's life had been shattered and there was a full expectation that if anyone deserved major compensation for the crash it would be him.

more critically hurt was an insurance salesman called David Green. He'd suffered serious fractures to his back and had lost almost all his blood.

When David emerged from a coma they broke the bad news to him. His back was so badly hurt he'd spend the rest of his life in a wheelchair. David had a strong Christian faith. He was a member of the Salvation Army but even his strong belief in God didn't stop him grieving badly over his personal loss of mobility.

"I came up to the gymnasium at the spinal unit one day", David recalls. "I'm a pretty tough guy but I burst into tears when I saw the other people sitting around with their disabilities and suddenly realised that I was now a cripple too."

David's rehabilitation was a painful affair. At one point, he had to lie perfectly still on his back for more than a month, so that a bad pressure sore could heal. Slowly he figured out what he was capable of doing. "One night I got really excited," he remembers now. "I woke up to realise that I'd rolled over by myself in bed."

Within a few weeks he was able to tie his own shoe laces. But that was about as far as David got. His back injury was apparently severe enough that he'd never be able to manage more than just a couple of steps on his own feet.

By this stage, with four dead and many injured, people were starting to talk seriously about whose fault the plane crash may have been. David's life had been shattered and there was a full expectation that if anyone deserved major compensation for the crash it would be him.

The system of Accident Compensation in New Zealand meant that David's rehabilitation was fairly comprehensive, but a firm of American lawyers was approaching all of the survivors from the crash offering them the chance to sue the manufacturers of the plane and the manufacturers of several parts on the aircraft which the lawyers said had not performed properly during the crash, leaving the manufacturers potentially liable.

The San Francisco-based lawyers told David Green that he would be the star witness in the case. "Because I was in a wheelchair," said David, "they said I would be the most compelling witness in an American court-room."

The lawyers told him that they fully expected that the American companies being sued would want to settle out of court and they said if David was the "visible face" of the intended court action, he alone could expect to be awarded around US$5 million at least. But something very profound had happened to David Green.

Rising Up

One weekend while he was praying about his predicament, David had a very strong impression. "It was just as if God was saying, 'I want you to forgive everybody involved in this crash,'" recalls David. "There seemed to be another part to what God was saying to me. The message was so clear: 'David, one day you're going to walk again'".

It was a decision that many people found difficult to comprehend. Many were urging David to take the money, even if he then gave it all away. But his mind was made up. "If I attempt to get money out of people, that will be tantamount to me not forgiving them and I don't think my heart will heal," David told me.

At the point at which we began our filming David was undergoing intensive physiotherapy at a gym for the disabled. With tortured, painful steps he tried to haul himself out of his wheelchair and take several steps around the gym floor. The experience would leave him exhausted and flushed.

His doctors were telling him not to expect very much. More as a journalistic exercise than anything else, we took David out in his wheelchair to show him what $5 million

The message was so clear: 'David, one day you're going to walk again.'

would buy. We showed him one of the finest boats at the best marina in town, we looked at half million dollar European cars, and we showed him around some lovely real estate.

With a good-natured grin David shook his head at all of the temptations. "Wheelchair ramps around this flash house would cost me way too much," he laughed.

Then, with a camera set up in a San Francisco's lawyer's office and another camera at David's home, we recorded the US attorney's last pleas to David to join in the legal action. They even quoted scripture at him to try to get underneath his skin. "You need to remember David," said the lawyer Terry Ford, "greater love hath no man than this that he lay down his life for the brethren."

David smiled a little on the other end of the phone. "I understand that Terry," he said kindly but firmly. "But the Bible also says vengeance is mine says the Lord and I will repay."

Eleven thousand kilometres away Terry Ford gave a slight smile and a shrug and acknowledged that he was up against some principles and personal beliefs that he just wasn't going to be able to topple. When David Green's story went on television, it was fascinating how many people found his principles admirable and worthy of considerable comment.

About two years later I met David again at a Salvation Army function in Wellington. "You need to go and see David," said a friend of mine pointing enthusiastically in David's direction. I wandered over to his table fully expecting to see the familiar shape of his wheelchair underneath the tablecloth. But there was no chair. David confidently got to his feet and leaned on two walking sticks.

He smiled a broad grin and I shook my head in amazement. "I'm still not quite there yet," said David. "Still using the chair a fair bit, but don't you reckon I've made progress?" What could I say? Here was a man who'd just got married again, didn't

Scriptural principles, when put to the test really do work.

have a bitter bone in his body and who still fully believed that a broken back was no obstacle to walking again.

Of all the stories I've done for "Extreme Close Up," that's been one of my favorites.

The Testing of Resolve

For forgiveness to work, it appears to me, there will sometimes come some severe testing. Have we forgiven or have we just tried to forget? David's story is now one I tell a lot as I remind people that the Bible's encouragement to us to be forgiving people does have some great real-life examples of how it can and does work.

The community went numb wondering who it might have been in their midst that could have done such an awful thing.

Sometimes you'll be talking to an audience in which there are people who are still full of rage over disasters that have befallen them or their loved ones. I'm reminded of an interview with a mother whose daughter died in the bombing of Pan Am flight 103 over Lockerbie in 1988.

The headline in the *Time* article about this woman is "Rage Makes Me Strong". She describes how she thinks it is imperative that she retains her anger. We've all seen how rage and bitterness warps the lives of people we know. Many of those people need to hear the stories of how others who've been faced with anguish as great as, or even greater than their own, have found that scriptural principles, when put to the test really do work.

The same year I reported on the story of David Green I also went to a unique twentieth anniversary remembrance. The event being remembered happened in November 1977 in a little suburb called Johnsonville, just outside New Zealand's capital city, Wellington.

A six-year-old girl called Lynley Stewart went missing from her home in the late afternoon. As the evening closed in, scores of local residents, students and police mounted a massive search for the little girl.

Lynley's parents, Keith and Rangi Stewart, were devout Christians and they looked at each sadly that evening because in the early hours of the previous morning Rangi, a woman who often had premonitions which proved to be true, had woken from a terrifying dream in which she'd seen her husband holding the lifeless body of one of their children.

Keith extended his hand to the other grieving father and gave his unconditional forgiveness. Rangi's dream was to come tragically true that evening, as Lynley's body was found underneath one of the classrooms at the Johnsonville Primary School. She'd been strangled, and there was the suspicion she'd been sexually assaulted. The community went numb wondering who it might have been in their midst that could have done such an awful thing.

The outcome of the police investigation was every bit as tragic as the discovery of what had happened to Lynley. They took a 14-year-old boy into custody – a young man who lived only a few houses away from the Stewarts.

"I knew the kid quite well," recalls Keith. "He used to come into the little shop we ran quite often, never gave him a second thought really." The boy's explanation of what had happened was confused, but there was no doubt he'd been responsible for Lynley's death. He was taken into custody although because of his age he could not be tried in court as an adult – simply sent to a boy's home where he was destined to spend the next few years.

The little community seethed with anger towards the boy. Keith was as heartbroken as any dad could be, but something quite profound happened in his own heart. "Something inside said that I had to go round to that boy's house and talk to his father."

At this stage the father of the boy responsible had himself been so grief-stricken by what his son had done, he'd taken to his bed feeling like his heart would break. The next thing he knew Keith Stewart was banging on his door. "I fully expected to see him there with an axe wanting to kill me and my family," the father told me at the time I was making the story.

"But there was something in his eyes that was altogether unexpected."

The way Keith tells the story he felt a divine push to go to the boy's father and offer a hand of forgiveness and prayer. "When I saw that poor man that night, he looked like he was only hours away from dying from his grief."

In what witnesses said was one of the most moving experiences of their lives Keith extended his hand to the other grieving father, gave his unconditional forgiveness and prayed for a healing to occur.

Twenty years after this all happened I was there at Lynley's graveside with Keith and other members of the family as they wondered what Lynley would have looked like aged 26. There were many tears – the feelings still acutely strong after two decades. But Keith has a presence and a calmness about him that is quite bewildering.

At the time I conducted the interviews with Keith, my own daughter Kate was the same age as Lynley was when she died. Even trying to imagine what Keith and his family had endured, was very hard for me. How on earth had he managed to summon up the ability to extend such complete forgiveness in the midst of such awful grief? Keith shook his head and suggested that this kind of attitude doesn't occur naturally, but has to be God-given.

But there was even more to the story. The young man who'd taken Lynley's life, did some hard time in a juvenile home. His life, and the lives of his family were obviously scarred forever by what had happened.

It transpired that many years later the young man, now grown, and having embraced Christianity, now with kids of his own, had heard Keith telling his story on the radio and had rung in after the show. A meeting was arranged. Lynley's father and Lynley's killer met together, shook hands and agreed as Christian brothers that no trace of hurt and anguish should remain.

The story's been written up, circulated around the world, and translated into several languages.

I firmly believe we've got to tell these stories as often as we can, to help bring some reality to our claims that God can and does move supernaturally over our needs.

Breathing Hope Into Hearers

Not everyone, or every situation, even in the Christian life, is so straightforward. There are complexities and layers to the big issues like forgiveness, and by no means is everyone's story the same.

But what I find "leaks out" of people most readily is hope, and we need to do whatever we can to put hope back. So often this is done through effective storytelling and the encouraging of people to believe that supernatural resources are available to those who'll dare to believe.

There it had been sitting, a real gem of a tale that I might never have got to hear.

Finding out about these stories can be as simple as being inquisitive enough to inquire of people when you meet them about what it is that's going on in their lives that best expresses God's love and providence.

I was teaching a group of young people a couple of years ago on the subject of communication. They were about to go into high schools to work in a highly effective mission to teenagers that's been running in New Zealand for several years called Teen Xtreme.

As I often do in these sessions I got the young people to pair up and tell each other in just a few words what had been their most stunning experience of God looking after them. When I asked some of the group to tell their stories to everyone a little later, one story in particular blew our minds.

A young man called Andrew, told us how he'd been riding his bike to university in the city of Christchurch a year or so earlier. "It was one of those real wet mornings," said Andrew, "and I felt the wheel of the bike go out from underneath me and the next thing I knew I was face down on the road looking back the way I'd come, with a car skidding to a halt only inches from my head."

Shaken, and sporting a few cuts and scrapes, Andrew got up and continued on his way to university on his slightly battered bike. When he got home that night and his Mum asked why he looked so beaten up, he told her about his experience earlier in the day. "She just burst into floods of tears immediately," Andrew told us.

Through her tears Andrew's Mum managed to explain the reason for her acute emotion. It turned out that only a few days earlier, this committed Christian woman had been woken out of an awful dream.

In the dream she'd seen Andrew on his bike taking a tumble on the exact bridge where he fell that morning. In the dream a car skidded and tried to avoid Andrew but had run over his head and killed him. "I came out into the lounge and prayed fervently for three hours," she told Andrew between sobs. "When I felt the burden lift and had a sense that God would spare your life, only then did I stop praying."

Andrew gave a slight grin as he finished his story. "I just want to encourage all of you," he said, "to know that the effectual fervent prayers of righteous people avail much."

The story really did leave us all quite breathless. And there it had been sitting, a real gem of a tale that I might never have got to hear about had I not been seeking to understand a bit more about the lives of the young people I was teaching.

I'm confident that everywhere we go people have these stories and the inquisitive side of us can always be looking for these jewels, ready to have them as powerful illustrative material for the talks we're giving.

–13–

The Remarkable Ones

"Therefore God is not ashamed to be called their God."
                                                    –Hebrews 11:16

Bunnie Walters was at one time, one of New Zealand's most respected and loved entertainers. He'd won the coveted title of Entertainer of the Year and had a beguiling gravely voice which lent itself to great live performances and a succession of hit records.

But in his 30's, Bunnie found himself staring at the world through the bottom of a glass. He blew his life apart on drink and drugs and became infamous around the club scene in Auckland. On one occasion as police were trying to get him to open the doors of his car so they could check for the drugs they suspected were inside, Bunnie blatantly held up his newborn baby to the window they were about to smash, then drove off to escape further attention.

"I was just fooling myself," Bunnie recalled as we walked along one of the streets where he used to stagger drunkenly, after downing an entire bottle of whiskey in the course of an afternoon. "I thought I was singing pretty well, but my life was just going down the toilet."

Bunnie became a Christian in a very powerful and sweeping way. Some swift and dramatic changes came about in his life and, given his charismatic personality and his way with people, he eventually found himself caught up in a very effective Christian ministry that spread its influence from New Zealand, all the way to the prison system in Canada.

It was at about this time that I started working with Bunnie on an "Extreme Close Up" story about his new life. I traveled to Winnipeg in

What a powerful thing it was to have someone be that open and acknowledge that he was not a plaster saint.

Canada to meet Bunnie and a fellow worker who were getting a very enthusiastic reception from the authorities at Stony Mountain Correctional Institution.

"I'll never forget the day the warden called us into his office," said Bunnie. "He just looked at us and said, 'I want to thank you boys, you've brought peace to this jail.'" What had happened at Stony Mountain was quite profound.

I discovered when I went there, the Christian principles that Bunnie and his mate had been teaching to the jail inmates had helped to drastically reduce inter-gang fighting in the jail. They had been asked to take their programme of reconciliation through Christian principles, to other jails across Canada.

On the face of it, this was a great success story. New Zealand men from humble beginnings making a great impact out in the world. Back home they had big plans too – to take over an entire vacant school, to help teach recovery to people diverted to their care from the criminal courts.

One night as Bunnie and I reminisced on the street in downtown Auckland, and completed our TV interviews, I said, "I want to ask you a very direct question while the camera's on."

"Sure," said Bunnie, "Anything." Not knowing what answer I'd get, I put it to him straight: "Bunnie, are you drug-free now?"

Bunnie thought for just the longest time. He nodded and I really wondered what was coming next. "Drug-free now," he repeated. "No, no I'm not."

"And you're still dealing with alcohol, aren't you?" I asked.

"Yes, that too."

The answer hung in the air, the honesty really unnerving. "But you're getting there?" I asked.

Bunnie nodded and then said gently, "Yes I am, yes I am."

And then quite spontaneously, in the strongest voice he could muster, he sang right there on Fort St powerful lines from a song by Christian artist Steve Apirana. The words go:

Even in the Bible people often moved from struggle to struggle while going from victory unto victory.

"It's not that I'm saying that I'm better than you, it's not that I'm judging everything that you do. Baby it's just, baby it's just, that I don't wanna go down that same old road no more."

It was an interesting moment for me. Here I was making a programme for secular television designed to convey the effectiveness of the Christian faith, and the hero of my story had openly admitted he was still really struggling. But in its own way it occurred to me immediately what a powerful thing it was to have someone be that open and acknowledge that he was not a plaster saint.

The more I thought about it, the more I realised how liberating it could be to have someone acknowledge their frailty for all to see. I feel so strongly whether the audience is Christian or non-Christian that our stories shouldn't be about image. We should be "real". In many ways, how much more delightful that God would use a man like Bunnie, flawed like we all are, to help do miracles around the world?

I believe it's important to include stories like this in our teaching. In my own early years as a Christian I grew up on story after story of God's deliverance and His bringing about complete [often very swift] victory for the person who was giving the testimony.

Years later I reckon it's still just as important that we hear the stories about God "coming through" and turning lives around and completely healing this or delivering that. But the older I get, the more I realise what complex beings we are, and that even in the Bible people often moved from struggle to struggle while going from victory unto victory.

I'm not suggesting we err on the side of telling stories where complete answers are not achieved, but we do need to tell the stories which reflect the way the grace of God can move and be applied even in the midst of our struggles.

Kate's Story

One of the most powerful stories I've been involved with of this ilk concerned the suicide of a young man who'd been a successful doctor and also a worship leader in his church. On the face of it, that maybe sounds like a story of failure and the inability of the young man concerned, to exercise enough faith to overcome his depression and suicidal tendencies.

"I saw Andrew arriving at the gates of heaven after he'd taken his life and there was God waiting for him."

After all, who's the winner when a young man like Andrew Dominikovich, aged only 34, leaves behind a promising career, not to mention a devoted wife, young son and a baby on the way? Indeed Andrew's funeral, and the grief expressed by those who spoke, was a wrenching thing to witness.

Here was a guy who'd stood up in the church, week after week, and encouraged others in song to touch God, believe in Him, and to overcome adversity.

When it was all over, however, we made a request of Andrew's widow, Kate. Knowing that she was a woman of uncommon faith, we asked whether we could follow her life on camera over the next year as she came to terms with being a Christian woman, deprived of her husband and many of her dreams.

The experience was in its own way uniquely powerful. Wrestling very early on with those enormous questions like, 'What does God think of a Christian person taking their own life?' Kate found some assurance that was quite breathtaking.

"It was as if I had a vision," says Kate. "I saw Andrew arriving at the gates of heaven after he'd taken his life and there was God waiting for him.

God told Andrew 'You've made a bad choice alright, but welcome home son, your room's ready for you.'"

It was exactly what Kate needed to experience to make sense of it all. "It was like God saying to Andrew that instead of taking the microscope to that one act of his life, God had always looked at Andrew as he does with any of us, through a benevolent wide angle lens."

The story we ultimately made about Andrew and Kate turned out to be one of our effective programmes. Kate has gone on to develop her own unique ministry out of the experience. She now talks to groups of people all around the country and is instrumental in leading people to God through the pain she's endured and the lessons she's learned.

I think the message is clear. If we only want to tell stories in which every post is a winning post, we deprive ourselves of those tales in which God does uniquely work through some things which initially may seem to be characterised by awful failure. I'm hearing more and more these days about church services where talks and intelligent interviews are being done on stages, using the stories of people who've endured great loss and stared failure in the face.

They may not have achieved a complete victory, but these stories in their own way bring huge liberation and understanding of God and His ways, and see the door opened to relationship between God and people in stunning ways.

Shari's Letter

Some stories sound almost too dramatic to be true. They're the tales, we might think nearly impossible, given the breathtaking nature of the subject.

But these are often the gems, if you can find them, which, when polished up, enable us to touch listeners in a very special way.

A few years back, I read one of the more chilling books I've ever picked up. It's called "Mindhunter," and it's about the grisly serial murder cases investigated by John Douglas – perhaps the most knowledgeable investigator on this subject in the Western world.

A fair chunk of the book is devoted to the investigation into a serial killer called Larry Gene Bell who was operating in the Southern States in the mid-eighties.

> **"It was such an extraordinary documentation of the character and courage of this young woman."**

On May 31st, 1985, Bell kidnapped 15 year old Shari Faye Smith from just outside her home near Columbia, South Carolina. Shari had been coming home from a nearby shopping centre, where she'd met her steady boyfriend, Richard. She was abducted at 3.38pm on a warm afternoon, just two days before she was due to sing the national anthem at the Lexington High School graduation.

Only minutes later, her father, Robert, found Shari's car at the head of the long driveway to the house. The door was open, the motor was running, and Shari's purse was lying on the seat. Panic-stricken, he called the Lexington County Sheriff's department.

The Smith family were committed Christians. Robert and Hilda had raised Shari and her siblings to know God, love Him and trust His word. That upbringing was to be pivotal in what unfolded over the next few days. Christian they may have been, but they anguished the way any family would under these circumstances.

They waited for some word, any word, even a ransom demand. Then they got a phone call. A man with a strangely distorted voice claimed he had Shari captive. The caller made no ransom demands, saying only, "You'll get a letter today." The family and the law officers became even more alarmed.

The letter came. John Douglas writes: "In all my years in law enforcement, with all of the horrible, almost unbelievable things I've seen, this is about the most heart wrenching."

Douglas published Shari's letter in his book because he says "it was such an extraordinary documentation of the character and courage of this young woman."

It was a two-page handwritten letter to the family from Shari. Written down the left side in capital letters was the phrase "GOD IS LOVE." Here's what it said:

6/1/85
3.10 am
Last Will and Testament

I love you Mommy, Daddy, Robert, Dawn and Richard and everyone else and all the other friends and relatives. I'll be with my father now, so please, please don't worry! Just remember my witty personality and great special times we all shared together. Please don't ever let this ruin your lives. Just keep living one day at a time for Jesus. Some good will come out of this. My thoughts will always be in and with you! I love you all so damn much. Sorry Dad, I had to cuss for once! Jesus forgive me. Richard sweetie – I really did and always will love you and treasure our special moments. I ask one thing though. Accept Jesus as your personal Saviour. My family has been the greatest influence of my life. Sorry about the cruise money. Some day please go in my place.

I am sorry if I ever disappointed you in any way, I only wanted to make you proud of me, because I have always been proud of my family. Mom, Dad, Robert and Dawn there's so much I want to say that I should have said before now. I love you!

I know y'all love me and will miss me very much, but if y'all stick together like we always did – y'all can do it.

Please do not become hard or upset. Everything works out for the good for those that love the Lord.

All my love always

Shari Smith [1]

Somewhere in the life of that girl and in the life of her family, was probably a great communicator.

Two days after Shari's family received her letter, a call from the killer let police know where they could find her body.

I never fail to be incredibly moved by this story, at several levels. Whenever I use Shari's story at a communications seminar, I always stress the amazing reality of true faith under fire. To any person who's tempted to believe that Christianity is all about "pie in the sky, by and by," remember Shari Smith.

To anyone who wonders whether it's worthwhile for a parent to persist in communicating Christ to your kids, remember Shari Smith.

And to those of you charged with communicating Jesus and making Him real, when you wonder if it's all worthwhile, remember Shari Smith.

Here's the truth – somewhere in the life of that girl and in the life of her family, was probably a great communicator – who knows, maybe several of them. Communicators who made the love and the power of God so real, that even when locked away with Larry Gene Bell, a man she knew would kill her, even facing death, Shari Smith had her feet so anchored on the Rock, she could encourage others not to lose heart.

Whatever you do as a communicator, make Jesus as real to your listeners, as someone did to Shari Faye Smith.

–14–

Retelling the Story

"Good teaching is one-fourth preparation and three-fourths theater."
–Gail Godwin

S it back for a moment and read something that ought to make you
think.

Some pastoral challenges are huge. Several years ago a church planter with a wide and influential ministry was approached by several concerned members of a large central city church with tales about the church that would make your hair stand on end. This leader was especially concerned because he'd planted the church in that town.

The story went like this. The deputation said our church is a mess. It now has splits in it that mean some people won't talk to others who were baptised by leaders whose technique and credentials are considered inferior. We have a lot of well-educated people in the church; university types, but they don't talk to the blue-collar workers, in fact they're openly sarcastic about people of what they regard as inferior education-al standards.

For all the brains in the church, there's a host of dumb things going on. The immorality that has made our city a subject of shame all round the country is now in the church too. We have to shake our heads sometimes they told the church planter – you know there's one guy who's seduced his stepmother away from his dad and they're actually living together. You'd think people in the church would be horrified. They're not. They tell jokes about it. They actually think it makes us broadminded and liberal. "Live and let live," they say.

Church services are a complete shambles. Everyone talks at the same time, no-one listens. Those who can pray in tongues babble away at the top of their voice, trying to outdo each other. I've seen visitors come to the door, shake their heads and walk away, totally confused. Just as well they don't stay. When the pot luck dinner starts, all the rich folks bring out their huge hampers of food and vintage wine and party up large in one corner, while the poor nibble on a bit of stale bread off in another part of the hall. There's no contact. The well-to-do stuff their faces then roll home drunk from church.

Perhaps it wouldn't be so bad if we at least knew what we believed. There are arguments over doctrine all the time, about really basic stuff like whether Jesus rose from the dead, and whether marriages should stay together.

We were going to come and see you earlier but we've been trying to sort out quite a bit of strife between a couple of members over a failed business venture that's gone sour and involved a bunch of people taking sides over who's right and who's wrong. It's in court now – a big lawsuit – with one guy claiming millions from the other. What a headache.

Do you think we have a solid future as a church, they asked the leader? Do you think you could give us a hand?

■■■■■

The above scenario is one I painted for a church recently when I was asked to speak at the induction service for a new pastor.

You probably recognised the church I was describing pretty early in the chapter. It is of course, the church at Corinth, details supplied by Paul in his first letter to that troubled congregation. I had to laugh a little when I got down from preaching that morning. A woman, with a deeply troubled face, tugged at my sleeve and asked, full of concern "Is it us? What's been going on here in the last couple of months!"

In one sense I suppose, Mission Accomplished! For at least one listener, I had achieved my goal – to introduce a bit of good old tension and release, and had made scriptural principles so real, she felt like it was happening in her own midst. This is part of the science I describe as "the great retell."

Making it Real All Over Again

I really believe part of the art of being a great storyteller is developing a style for retelling Bible stories, or bringing them into modern idiom in ways that really connect with an audience.

John Ortberg, teaching pastor at Willow Creek Community Church is, I believe, one of the best exponents of "the great retell."

Earlier, I mentioned how John quoted the marshmallow-temptation research in his talk about the attitude of commitment.

In the same teaching, he relates with considerable skill the story of how Abraham found a wife for his son Isaac.

"And Then Some"

I want to give you three words today, but they are not original with me. I first heard them a long time ago, and these three words can change your work and transform your life. I think they are the ultimate challenge for human beings.

The three words are "and then some". Do what is expected as minimally required – and then some. Become an "and then some" kind of person. Do whatever your hand finds for you to do with all of your strength.

I want to tell you a story from the Bible about an "and then some" kind of person. This story is found in the Book of Genesis at the very beginning of scripture. As it starts, Abraham – whom some of you know was the father of Israel and the beginning of the nation of Israel – is at this point an old man. His wife had died and it was time for his son Isaac to be married.

This was a real important deal. The whole future of the people of Israel relied on this marriage, because they were all going to be descendants of Isaac. Abraham had to find a great wife. She had to be someone who could be the mother of these children, raise the offspring and begin to shape a whole people.

How was Abraham going to find a wife for Isaac? There were no computer dating services in those days, no singles bars and no news papers where Isaac could write a personal ad – "attractive nomad with excellent prospects searching for female who likes to travel." They couldn't do it that way.

They had a custom in those days, and the custom was that the parent would arrange the marriage for the kid. The parent would go out, scour the countryside, find a real good candidate, come home and say to the kid, "This is who you are going to marry." The older I get and my kids get, the more sensible that biblical custom sounds to me.

Here is what Abraham did. He was old and not far from death, so he called his most trusted servant, a man most likely named Eliezer. Abraham explained, "My time is almost done, and I am going to die soon. My son, the future of Israel, needs a wife, and she needs to be a person of flawless character. She needs to be someone who can be faithful to God and one with Isaac."

Eliezer accepted this commission and assembled a caravan of ten camels, laden with gifts. He knew that he was going to have to give them to the family of the girl that he would take away. He went to a city called Nahor, and had the camels kneel down while he stood by a well outside the town. Eliezer began to pray, since he didn't know what else to do. He said "God grant me success on this mission. I need a sign from you that you are in this, so this is what I ask. When the young women come here to this well, I will say, "Would you get me some water?" Let one of them say, "I will get a drink for you, and water for your camels as well." That will be a sign that she is the one."

In the East in those days, hospitality was taken very seriously. It was often a matter of life and death for travelers, and was a sign of character. Eliezer waited. Among the people coming and going was a young woman *named Rebekah. The text says that she was a woman of pure character and very fair to look upon. The phrase used in the Hebrew was "she was a righteous babe". That's a loose translation.*

When Rebekah came, she lowered her jar into the well, and gave it to Eliezer to drink. When he finished drinking, she said, "I will draw water for your camels, too, until they have finished drinking."

Here's the kicker. When a group of us went to Israel a couple of months ago, we saw camels. Some of us rode on them. Do you have any idea how much one thirsty camel can drink? One camel at the end of a journey can drink up to thirty gallons of water. Do you remember how many camels were in the caravan? Do the math.

Here was a guy standing by a well, who asked the girl, a total stranger, "Can I have a drink of water?" She handed the drink of water to him and then said, "Sure! I will also pull up, by myself, another 300 gallons of water for your camels." This was a girl with some serious biceps.

Here's the story. Rebekah did everything that reasonably could have been expected of her – and then some. It's the "and then some" that made all the difference. It changed her life and history, because she went on to marry Isaac and began a great adventure with God. [1]

The beauty of the way Ortberg tells the story is wrapped up in several key concepts. As a journalist reading the script, I notice vital storytelling techniques, which help the listeners remain in rapt attention, as they hear this message.

- The sentences are short and to the point

- There is great humour, in today's vernacular and using today's images, interwoven with a story that is more than 3500 years old

- There is application of the "and then some" principle right at the out-set ["Do what is expected as minimally required – and then some. Become an "and then some" kind of person. Do whatever your hand finds for you to do with all of your strength."]

- There is the power of the question [How is Abraham going to achieve this?]

- There is pertinent and relevant information drawn from personal experience [the stomach capacity of a camel].

- There's clear evidence Ortberg has sat and thought about the implications of one woman drawing water for ten camels

As you see, there's way more to this business of talk preparation than just sitting down for an hour and a half, throwing a few scriptures together, and linking it all up with a bit of general exhortation.

Another Night With the Frogs

Ortberg really is a master at this kind of storytelling.

Here's how he tackles the subject of Procrastination, using a well-trod passage from Exodus to make his point.

I want to suggest to you what might be the single most dangerous word in the English language. It's found in Exodus chapter eight. In this part of the Bible the Israelites have been living in slavery for a long time, for centuries, and they want freedom. But there's one of the great labour-management conflicts of all time. From the labour end, the Israelites have a very bad contract. Work and then die!

And Moses is their top guy, but he doesn't have much leverage, and the rank and file is a little shaky. Management is represented by Pharaoh and he is a hard-line negotiator. So God gives Moses some very powerful bargaining chips known as the ten plagues. To kind of level the playing field.

In one of them the water in Egypt turns to blood. The whole Nile is filled with blood. Fish die, the stench spreads through the country. Other plagues involve gnats, flies, locusts, boils and in the midst of this, one of the most memorable plagues is written about in Exodus eight, starting in verse six, and this account has the key word that I want to focus on tonight in Pharaoh's response to Moses.

Aaron stretched out his hand over the waters of Egypt and the frogs came up and covered the land. But the magicians did the same thing by their secret arts. They also made frogs come up on the land of Egypt. Pharaoh summoned Moses and Aaron and said "Pray to the Lord to take the frogs away from me and my people and I will let your people go to offer sacrifices to the Lord."

Moses said to Pharaoh "I leave to you the honour of setting the time for me to pray for you and your officials and your people, that you and your houses may be rid of the frogs, except for those that remain in the Nile. "Tomorrow," Pharaoh said.

There's the word. Tomorrow.

You want to ask Pharaoh one question. What are you thinking! Get the picture. The frogs are out of control. Look at verse three. The Nile will teem with frogs. They will come up into your palace, and into your bedroom and onto your bed, into the houses of your officials and on your people, and into your ovens and kneading troughs.

Pharaoh can't even back his chariot out of the garage without killing a hundred frogs. His pizza is covered with frogs. If his home is anything like mine his wife and oldest daughter have been standing on chairs screaming since the plague began. His youngest daughter has run out of jars in which to collect and accidentally suffocate the frogs.

The frogs are everywhere, but when Moses offers to get rid of them, what's Pharaoh's response?

Tomorrow.

Does he enjoy frogs' legs? Is the sound of his shrieking daughters music to his ears? Is he tired of sleeping alone? What could possibly motivate the man to wait until tomorrow if he could resolve the problem today? Why spend another night with the frogs? [2]

The phrase "another night with the frogs" then becomes the touchstone for the rest of Ortberg's message, as he confronts his listeners about the dangers of procrastination. But there's more.

By dangling the thought in front of us, at the beginning, that he knows the most dangerous word in the English language, he immediately grabs our attention and gets our minds working. We're probably thinking of words like 'war' and 'death' and 'hatred'. What a good storyteller like Ortberg knows is the same secret that's being used by writers of great novels and movie scripts for years.

You don't give away the total premise of your presentation at the outset. The great part is that people love a bit of mystery and will stay with you on the journey to find out where it is you're really going.

■■■■■

There is sheer magic when a good storyteller can go into a Bible text and bring it to life in new ways. One of the most memorable examples of this, that I ever heard, was during a stop at a tiny church in Grand Junction, Colorado, more than 20 years ago.

Showdown in the Temple

A preacher was addressing a bunch of kids in their teens and trying to explain how Jesus Christ breaks down barriers in people's lives. He used the story of Jesus going into the temple and clearing out the money changers. He'd evidently researched his subject extensively and was able to tell us just what the system was as Jewish worshippers came to the temple to make their sacrifices.

"Imagine having hiked for miles," he said "with your little lamb dragging along behind you on a piece of rope. You were not only conscious of the journey but of the things you'd done wrong and how you were going to have to wait in the heat just to be able to tell God you were sorry."

The preacher roamed back and forth across the stage with energetic hand movements and passion in his voice describing the queues and lines you had to endure as you first had your lamb inspected, then rejected on some spurious grounds, then there was the line to buy a new lamb, only to discover that your money was no good and needed to be changed into temple coinage.

He drew you into his tale of rip-off and frustration at the hands of temple inspectors and moneychangers and got you to the point where you were really personally fuming with indignation. Right then, he brings the hero into the story.

"There's a commotion over there in the corner. Can you hear it? Some guy has got hold of a moneychanger by his collar and is shaking him till his eyes bulge. Now what's he doing? He's leaning over and picking up some of the ropes that have fenced people off from the temple and been part of the system of rip-off and exploitation. Now what's he doing? He's making a whip. Wow, what's going on? Jesus is whopping on them dudes!"

By now, as you can imagine, we in the audience are totally involved. It's classic light and shade as the preacher's voice gets real quiet and dramatic for a moment and asks us to picture one last scene. "One of those money changers, confused and dazed, is down on the floor, scrabbling for his coins, trying to find where they went, trying to shovel them back into his bag. Behind him a shadow is looming. He turns around and looks into those eyes. It's the Son of God and He's not very happy!"

The preacher then paints a last picture of glorious liberation – of all the barriers gone, of all those who were standing in the way of ordinary worshippers, sent scurrying out of the Temple.

And now there's just Jesus and the sick and the needy and the desperate, and He beckons them towards Him. No sacrifice needed now. No contortions of righteousness. Just a chance to be with the One who has reclaimed the temple for its rightful purpose. The God, who still today, goes on breaking down barriers between Himself and His people.

How many talks about generalities I must have heard over the years, but how few have stayed in my mind with such clarity.

Painting With Words

We are an extremely visual generation. So much of the information and window on the world we now get comes off screens.

But in reality people have always been visual, and the best storytellers have always made an impact by getting people to imagine scenes that are skillfully painted with a word brush.

The related skill is to look at the detail of stories in scripture and try to pick out those fascinating details, which make for irony, pathos and discovery.

A great example of this is to be found at the end of John's Gospel, where Peter and other disciples have gone back fishing even after Jesus has risen from the dead. The story of Jesus' patience with his disciples at this time is very touching. They come back from fishing to find him on the beach and there's a fire kindled and breakfast is under way. Astonishing enough to stop and think that here was the Son of God sitting down and preparing their meal for them, but there's another deal buried in here.

There's Peter wandering up the beach and what's the smell that fills his nostrils? It's a charcoal fire and there's Jesus next to it. When was the last time, you might ask yourself, that Peter smelled burning charcoal? Might it not have been the fire at which he warmed his hands shortly before he denied Jesus not once but three times?

So it's a tender moment, full of meaning, as Jesus comes back to not just remind him that he did deny his Master, but more importantly that the Master was so full of grace, he was prepared to extend a hand of forgiveness and the chance for a fresh start.

You capture these moments for people by placing yourself in the middle of the story and imagining the scene, allowing yourself to indulge your senses for a moment, maybe even to taste the fish and smell the fire. The stories are all there in the pages of the Bible, ready to be experienced all over again.

–15–

Quote Great Things

"Whatever is true, whatever is noble, whatever is right, whatever is pure, whatever is lovely, whatever is admirable – if anything is excellent or praiseworthy – think about such things."
–Philippians 4:8

There's no doubt about it. People want to be inspired. One of the stories we did for our "Extreme Close Up" TV series was about a man of strong Christian character who was dying of cancer. He'd received hundreds of cards and letters from people encouraging him on his journey.

We finished our programme on his life, with him reading the words of a poem he'd been sent. The effect of these words on viewers was electrifying. Scores of people wanted a copy.

In their own way, these lines are just a great way of restating many Biblical principles with which we are familiar. Ideas like " Where, O death is your victory? Where O death, is your sting?" are wrapped up in the poem:

"Cancer is so limited, it cannot cripple love, it cannot shatter hope, it cannot corrode faith, it cannot eat away peace, and it cannot destroy confidence. It cannot kill friendship, it cannot shut out memories, it cannot silence courage and it cannot invade the soul. It cannot reduce eternal life, it cannot quench the spirit and it cannot lessen the power of the resurrection."

I've long been a believer in studying the lives of great people and extracting quotes from their speeches.

Theodore Roosevelt once delivered memorable words that are powerful encouragement for those who sometimes find themselves the subject of criticism.

"It is not the critic who counts, nor the man who points out where the strong man stumbled or where the doer of deeds could have done them better. The credit belongs to the man who is actually in the arena; whose face is marred by dust and sweat and blood; who strives valiantly. Who errs and comes short again and again; who knows the great enthusiasms, the great devotions. Who spends himself in a worthy cause. Who at the best knows in the end the triumph of high achievement; who at the worst, if he fails, at least fails while daring greatly, so that his place will never be with those timid souls who know neither victory nor defeat."

Such quotes make a great follow on when preaching on the great chapters and exploits of faith.

Journalling

I have found that one of the most valuable gifts you can give to yourself as a preacher/teacher, is the practice of keeping a journal/scrapbook in which you can jot or paste inspirational things you pick up as you go through life. I browsed my 1997 journal recently, and got thrilled all over again.

Ponder one entry, from Jim Elliott, the martyred missionary, not too long before his life was taken.

"I walked out on the hill just now. It is exalting, delicious, to stand embraced by the shadow of a friendly tree with the wind tugging at your coattail and the heavens hailing your heart. To gaze and glory, and give yourself again to God. What more could a man ask? Oh, the fullness, pleasure and sheer excitement of knowing God on earth! I don't care if I never raise my voice again for Him. If only I may love Him, please Him, if only I may see Him, touch His garments and smile into His eyes."

If we think creatively, words like these can be used to help restate great Bible truths, and hey, they're not bad on their own, right?

The diaries of great men and women of God are always going to produce an abundance of inspiration. I note in my journal, not long after the words of Jim Elliott, the following observations of David Brainerd, another Christian with a huge heart:

"In the silences I make in the midst of the turmoil of life, I have appointments with God. From these silences I come forth with spirit refreshed, and with a renewed sense of power. I hear a Voice in the silences, and become increasingly aware that it is the Voice of God. O how comfortable is a little glimpse of God!"

Beyond Brainerd, in my journaling that year, I found there was one page that had become particularly well thumbed, as I now look back. It was an excerpt from a very passionate address given to the Leadership Summit at Willow Creek by Bill Hybels.

I think the reason it was there in my journal is clear.

"If leaders don't have clear callings and passionate visions, if leaders don't make fierce commitments to God to carry them out in a self-sacrificial way, to the point of death, if necessary, if leaders don't give off an aroma to those around them, which says "God's at the root of this, and I'm serious about it, and I'm committed and I'll pay whatever price," followers never ignite, they never get infected with the vision, they never get their hearts set ablaze, and they never cross over that line and they never say, "Then I'm with you!"

Confused trumpet players, playing dissonant, dispassionate music, just winds up with listeners shaking their heads and going about doing whatever it was they were doing before. And this is the prevailing condition of Christendom."

Throw that quote into a talk on leadership sometime as an illustrative device, and that brings the crowd to attention!

Reading on a little further in my collection I find the daily prayer of Mother Teresa.

"Dearest Lord, may I see you today and every day in the person of your sick, and whilst nursing, minister to you.

Though you hide yourself behind the unattractive disguise of the irritable, the exacting, the unreasonable, may I still recognise you and say: "Jesus, my patient, how sweet it is to serve you."

Lord give me this seeing faith, then my work will never be monotonous. I will ever find joy in humouring the fancies and gratifying the wishes of all poor sufferers.

O beloved sick, how doubly dear you are to me, when you personify Christ; and what a privilege is mine to be allowed to tend you.

Sweetest Lord, make me appreciative of the dignity of my high vocation, and its many responsibilities. Never permit me to disgrace it by giving way to coldness, unkindness or impatience.

And, O God, while you are Jesus, my patient, deign also to be to me a patient Jesus, bearing with my faults, looking only to my intention, which is to love and serve you in the person of each of your sick.

Lord, increase my faith, bless my efforts and work, now and for evermore."

Dare To Be a Poet

Never be afraid of majestic language, great words, and even poetry. I have found that even the mere reciting of the stunning words of a hymn, can have a near instant effect on listeners, especially as you draw to the close of a message.

It's the same principle you find at the singing of an anthem, or the reciting of inspirational sayings. There's something in most of us that responds to a great sense of occasion. There is a huge lifting of the soul that occurs in the process of declaration. We respond with our heart just as much as with our mind.

I'm told that the ancient Romans, who were big on oratory, used to have two distinct types of speechmaker. One was the guy you'd go out to hear for an evening's entertainment. The kind of talk you go out to hear that gets you saying on the way home "Hmm, nice speech."

The other kind of speechmaker was the fellow whose sole job was to put fire into the belly of troops before they marched off to battle. He'd stand in front of the army, and speak so powerfully and inspire such motivation, those Roman soldiers would be fit to mow down anything that stood in their path!

I guess it's the same principle of a coach in the locker room before the big game starts.

Ponder the powerful sentiments in the following poem, which paints a beautiful picture of the Father, cheering us from the sidelines as we run "the race set before us."

THE RACE

Quit! Give Up! You're beaten!
They shout at me and plead.
There's just too much against you now
This time you can't succeed.

And as I start to hang my head
In front of failure's face
My downward fall is broken,
By the memory of a race.

And hope re-fills my weakened will
As I recall that scene
For just the thought of that short race
Rejuvenates my being.

It was a children's race – young boys, young men
How I remember well!
Excitement – sure! But also fear,

It wasn't hard to tell.

They all lined up, so full of hope
Each thought to win the race
To try for first, or if not that,
At least take second place.

And fathers watched from off the side,
Each cheering for his son
And each boy hoped to show his dad
That he would be the one.

Well, the whistle blew and off they went
Young hearts and hopes afire,
To win and be the hero there
Was each young boy's desire.

One boy in particular
Whose dad was in the crowd
Was running near the lead and thought,
My dad will be so proud!

But as they speeded down the field
Across the shallow dip
The little boy who thought to win,
Lost his step, and slipped.

Trying hard to catch himself,
His hands flew out to brace
And mid the laughter of the crowd,
He fell flat on his face.

So down he fell, and with him, hope
He couldn't win it now
Embarrassed, sad, he only wished,
To disappear, somehow.

But as he fell, his dad stood up,

And showed an anxious face
Which to the boy so clearly said,
Get up! and win the race!

He quickly rose – no damage done
Behind a bit, that's all
And he ran with all his mind and might
To make up for his fall.

So anxious to restore himself
To catch up and to win
His mind went faster than his legs
He slipped and fell again.

He wished then he had quit before
With only one disgrace.
"I'm hopeless as a runner now,
I shouldn't try to race."

But in the laughing crowd he searched
And found his father's face
That steady look which said to him
Get up! And win the race!

So up he jumped, to try again
Ten yards behind the last.
"If I'm to gain those yards," he thought
"I've got to move real fast."

Exerting everything he had,
He gained eight or ten
But trying so hard to catch the lead
He slipped and fell again.

Defeat... He lay there silently,
A teardrop from his eye
There's no sense running anymore
Three strikes, I'm out. Why try?

The will to rise had disappeared,
All hope had fled away
So far behind, so error-prone
A loser all the way.

I've lost, so what's the use, he thought.
I'll live with my disgrace.
But then he thought about his dad
Who soon he'd have to face.

Get up!... an echo sounded low.
Get up and take your place!
You were not meant for failure here,
Get up and win the race!

With borrowed will, get up, it said.
You haven't lost at all.
For winning is no more than this:
To rise each time you fall.

So up he rose to run once more,
And with a new commit
He resolved that win or lose,
At least, he wouldn't quit.

So far behind the others now,
The most he'd ever been
Still, he gave it all he had,
And ran as though to win.

Three times he'd fallen, stumbling
Three times he'd rose again
Too far behind to hope to win
He still ran to the end.

They cheered the winning runner,
As he crossed the line, first place
Head high, and proud, and happy

No falling, no disgrace.

But when the fallen youngster
crossed the line in last place
The crowd gave him the greater cheer
For finishing the race.

And even though he came in last
With head bowed low, unproud
You would have thought he'd won the race,
To listen to the crowd.

And to his dad, he sadly said
"I didn't do so well."
"To me, you won," his father said
"You rose each time you fell."

And now when things seem dark and hard
And difficult to face,
The memory of that little boy
Helps me in my own race.

For all of life seems like that race
With ups and downs and all
And all you have to do to win,
Is rise each time you fall.

Quit! Give up! You're beaten!
They still shout in my face.
But another voice inside me says
Get up! and win the race.

–16–

Putting It All Together

So what have we learned about being better storytellers? I said right at the outset that part of my passion for stories arises out of being a journalist. But I think before I was a journalist I was just naturally inquisitive and really interested about ordinary people and their lives. I reckon this is a prerequisite for improving our storytelling ability and style.

If you're not that much interested in people and the world around you, you probably won't extend the borders of your curiosity very far. My strong suggestion to you is that you put yourself in situations regularly where you can hear people's stories and become entranced by the variety of experience and teaching potential there is in those around you.

The Diary in the Plane Wreck

I once asked a man after a church service rather innocently whether he'd done anything interesting that weekend. "Why sure," he said. "I went to a pretty interesting memorial service yesterday up at a beach near where I live." It was quite a long story but the import of it was fascinating. It turned out that his grandfather, a missionary, had been back on leave from his overseas posting, and had died in a plane crash.

A scorched sheet of paper blew out of where the plane had been wrecked.

The man telling me the story said that his uncle, another son of the fellow who died, had been devastated by his dad's death and had been sitting down near where the plane had crashed, asking God why on earth something so terrible could have happened to a godly man. A small wind

The man who'd died in the plane knew somehow in his spirit, that the end of his life was near. had arisen and blown a scorched sheet of paper out of where the plane had been wrecked. The paper wrapped itself around the legs of the man sitting morosely beside the runway.

Believe it or not, the piece of paper was the very last page of the missionary's diary – a page on which he'd written out in full a verse of scripture which spoke about people not grieving when others die, but living on in the expectation of meeting them again in heaven.

The implication was clear: the man who'd died in the plane knew somehow in his spirit, that the end of his life was near and now in quite a remarkable way was able to send a message of encouragement from beyond the grave to a young man whose life, when he picked up the sheet of paper, would be powerfully impacted for good. With a slight shrug of his shoulders the man talking to me said, "So that's what I did yesterday. What about you."

I'm almost laughing now as I recall the incident. What amazing things you discover if only you ask questions!

In summary then I'd like to leave you with a checklist of things that I think are really important for those of us who desire to be expositors of God's truth and tellers of His stories.

1. Be relentlessly but politely inquisitive. The truth is, that no matter how shy people may appear, many of them really do love talking about themselves. Encourage people to open up about their lives. It's important that you do this out of a genuine interest and that you don't just stand there with your head buried in a notebook writing furiously the whole time they're talking.

2. Much of what you hear can be committed to memory and the detail checked later if necessary. But do keep that notebook tucked at the back of your Bible, perhaps, or carry one with you to note down stories that you hear that appeal to you. You may even find a small cassette recorder is worth making part of your briefcase. You may be

interested to know that much of this book was written as I drove on long car journeys and spoke into my dictaphone!

3. Be a wide and avid reader. Some people almost make it a mark of faith that they only read their Bible or certain religious books. I think that's a pretty narrow approach, and you will soon find yourself getting out of touch with the kind of questions and issues that characterise the lives of unchurched people, who after all are supposed to be our harvest field. I think it's valuable to be taking in at least one or two news magazines like *Time*, *Newsweek* or something similar each month. The correspondents for these publications can help provide you with a window on the world.

4. If you don't already have a fantastic filing system at home I suggest you get one of those accordion-type boxes with an index on it that allows you to file clippings and ideas as you accumulate them. Become a keen collector of newspaper and magazine articles that tell the kind of stories you know you might be able to use one day. These days so much of the hard work has gone out of this kind of thing with the advent of computers. You may find a filing system in your computer offers a more convenient way to do this. But given the wide variety of sources I suggest you access, I think an indexed folder of some sort is a great idea.

5. Listen to great storytellers. I'm not suggesting that you go for straight out imitation, but access whatever you can from good teachers like ones I've mentioned in this book, and study the way they retell stories, the way they make biblical narrative come to life, and the way they manage to mix scripture and example.

6. Don't be afraid to incorporate real stories into your messages by having the stories actually told by a live person or on video. I saw Rick Warren from Saddleback Community Church in California do this very effectively at a conference a few years ago, and I gather it's a regular practice of his.

Right in the middle of teaching other pastors about how to bring great messages, he plucked from his musical team behind him, a man who was obviously expecting the call, and who gave a short and powerful account of how he remembered his alcoholic father trying to break down the door of their home with an axe. Sometimes a short, pithy interview with such a person will do the trick.

Bringing a real story right at that moment into the middle of his talk was one of the most effective ways of using a personal story I've ever seen. A video clip can sometimes do the same job, but it's important that the clip be of good quality and that the technical side of weaving it into your message should be as seamless as possible.

7. Exercise some care and forethought about the kind of stories that you tell. I've been witness to and a participant in some really embarrassing experiences over the years when it comes to being overzealous about storytelling. I think one of the crucial mistakes that people make is telling stories about their own family without thinking of the sensitivities they might be arousing or the discomfort they may cause.

When it comes to spouse and children I would urge caution and seeking of permission. In the desperate search for a sermon illustration you can do great harm. I learned this in another way to my personal cost a number of years ago in using an illustration I should have thought much harder about.

Several years earlier there'd been a devastating airline crash over the Antarctic in which several hundred New Zealanders had died. I should have recalled quite clearly the words of somebody at the time, that everyone in our country knew at least someone who'd been on that aircraft, such is the small size of New Zealand.

It should, therefore, have come as no surprise to me that, shortly after I started using in my talk, an aspect of the crash – the role of incorrect navigational co-ordinates in the disaster – that a woman began quietly sobbing at the back of the meeting. It turned out that her mother had been on the plane.

Can you imagine how awful I felt? Now it wasn't, of course, possible for me to check out before I gave that talk to ensure that nobody in the meeting would be so closely affected. But a little bit of common sense might have made all the difference. Perhaps there are some places, depending on where you are, that it would better not to go!

There's a related point here: don't use stories that you've heard about local happenings without checking details. Sometimes people will pass information to you about some great thing they've heard and the temptation is to immediately incorporate it into a talk as illustrative material.

I've been caught badly, more than once, passing on details of something that members of my audience knew way more about than I did, and it turned out they had to correct me on important points. That's really embarrassing. My practice now invariably is the same procedure that I would follow as a journalist: check, check, and then check again if necessary.

8. Never be afraid to give credit to where you got the story from. Sometimes we might think we'd come across as far more inspired if we made it sound like this story was all our own. But don't be fooled, the world is a very small place now and stories can circle the globe in seconds.

If you attribute, that tells audiences who are tuned in, very important things about you. It speaks volumes about your integrity for a start. So if you get a great tale out of a book, do the writer or the source the same courtesy that you would expect if somebody picked up some of your original material.

9. Spend time immersing yourself in the Bible stories that you're going to teach on. Make sure you allow room for the story to "breathe". Try and imagine what it would have been like, for example, for Peter, the tough fisherman, making his decision to get out of the boat in a Force 10 gale and walk towards Jesus on that tempestuous sea. When you've read the story, sit back, close your eyes, and just allow yourself the liberty of   re-living the emotions, motivations and expectations of the participants. You may be amazed at what comes out.

Telling Stories Well

There's a trap that's easy to fall into, even if you've selected a good story to use as an illustration. Like me, you've probably heard plenty of good preachers who've tried to use a story that has enormous potential, only to have it fall somewhat sort in terms of its power and effect on an audience.

Many of the mistakes we make in this regard can be easily corrected. From my observations of good and not-so-good story tellers over the years, I've put together what I consider to be some useful tips.

1. Always use a story that provides you with a good bridge to the point you really want to make. Sometimes speakers get a hold of a story that is personally appealing to them, but then their attempt to link it to the general thrust of their talk becomes incredibly laboured and difficult, because they either haven't properly thought out their transition, or the story is just off the mark in terms of their subject matter.

   A good rule of thumb is that a great story provides an easy transition. Some speakers work at this process incredibly hard. I have a preacher friend in California who says he'll sometimes spend more than an hour pacing up and down on the floor of his study thinking of just the right words to transition from his story to the rest of his content.

   Every now and then it's not a bad idea to try out the linkage between your story and your subject by giving it a "dry run" on somebody whose judgment you trust.

2. Speakers often read too much of a story and it goes on for way too long. Lots of the good stories you'll come across may need some editing. One good way of going through the editing process is to use a highlighter pen to simply bring out those portions of a written story that you want to use in your presentation. This process can be greatly enhanced by becoming very familiar with the story, and being able if possible to relate a good portion, either from memory or by giving sharp ad lib linkages between the portions of the story you really want to bring out.

3. Get the story into your heart as much as possible so that you're not just reading it off a piece of paper; it's you telling a story that you actually feel quite strongly about. This doesn't mean there's anything wrong with working from a manuscript, or reading things out to ensure accuracy. It just means that you ought to be familiar enough with the text that you can make that all important eye contact with your audience on a fairly regular basis during the telling of the story and you thereby have them feel some of what you feel about the tale you are relating.

4. Don't be afraid to use the "active voice" during the telling of the story. See if there's an opportunity there to effectively act out the part of a couple of the people in the story, using different inflections in your voice to create a sense of dialogue. This may help the flow and the impact of your story.

5. It would be possible to write a whole book, and I guess someone has, on the whole question of how you use your voice. Suffice to say for our purposes in this book, that if you can introduce some light and shade into your presentation, you undoubtedly become a storyteller that people will warm to.

In other words, when it's appropriate, use a pause and don't say anything for two to three seconds, maybe even longer, to let some of the impact of an important part in the story sink in. It's also okay to get real quiet occasionally and take your voice down to something approaching a whisper, or up to the level of a manageable shout, to help dramatise what you're saying. Don't overact, but don't be afraid to bring some performance values to what you're doing.

6. All of the above comments lead to one other very important observation. It's when you speak from your heart, about things you know, you've experienced or which have touched you deeply, that you are likely to be at your most compelling. It's also when you will often be at your most credible because you know whereof you speak.

The flip side of this, of course, is that some people, in pursuit of this value, can end up scouring the barrel of their own experiences and can finish up talking about things which are not terribly interesting stories at all!

But it's those moments in your life, when maybe you suffered and learned something through your suffering, where you made a mistake and had to put it right, or where you had to dig deep into your faith and find strength for a particular trial, that you will very often find yourself resonating with your audience.

–17–

Trends – Final Thoughts

"Fifty seven channels, and nothing on."
–Bruce Springsteen

"Turn my eyes away from worthless things; preserve my life according to your word."
–Psalm 119:37

On one of those interminable airplane journeys, I read something depressing about the future of the industry in which I earned my living for twenty-five years. It was a series of predictions about how television and other media would likely develop into the 21st century.

Todd Gitlin, professor of culture, journalism and sociology at New York University, had written his piece, "Pop goes the culture," for a weekly news magazine, and he did not see a noble future for the media.

"Driven by panic as much as rational planning, media conglomerates will try out one sensation after another. The taste for sensation cuts across all cultural lines. Popular culture will go on delivering short bursts of feeling that are, in a sense, more chemical than emotional. They are meant to tickle the ribs with gags, or to thrill, but not to overwhelm or cultivate... the kinetic style is what audiences will expect: one microintensity after another." [1]

Gitlin wrote that piece well before many of the so-called "reality" programmes were even on our screens, and in hindsight, I find his words prophetic.

There's a phrase I sometimes use to myself when shaking my head over the depressing numbers of people shown by the ratings to

"The kinetic style is what audiences will expect: one microintensity after another."

People are starting to wake up to the notion that God is worth another shot.

have watched some trash show on network TV. I think, to some extent we've "poisoned the well" for viewers – in other words, they've been fed a diet of visual junk food, and now many are hooked.

So is it a depressing time to be a communicator? In some ways, yes, but in other ways I find that the darker the background, the easier it is for a real gem to shine. As I talk to my unchurched friends, I find in many, a more acute hunger for substance than there was in previous years. Some Christians get all fired up about the amount of literature around that focuses on spirituality – as if the proliferation of books about angels and "new age" phenomena is a sign of really dark times.

I'm inclined to take a more optimistic view. Could it be that people are just plain hungry? I think the recent stunning secular acclaim for Bruce Wilkinson's "The Prayer of Jabez," the #1 New York Times Bestseller, is a case in point.

Maybe now that people have figured out that the "big promises" of the late 20th century – science, wealth, therapy and entertainment – did not deliver heaven on earth, people are starting to wake up to the notion that God is worth another shot!

As I write this final chapter, the latest survey from a big project known as the New Zealand Values Study has just been published. It's found that the trend towards spiritual awareness in our country continues to grow. This morning's newspaper story says:

Sin is back. Not in our behaviour, but in our beliefs. A survey of New Zealanders' values shows that belief in sin has almost doubled since 1985, and that spirituality is on the rise. [2]

Survey chief Dr Alan Webster commented:

"It seems to be a reflection of the greater seriousness that has struck modern people about the many very frightening and bad things going on in the world, and they don't mind using the word sin to explain them." While

51 percent of those aged 60 and over believed in sin, it rose to 64 percent for those aged 31-40, suggesting a generational reaction against the youth culture of the 1960's.

I think this is a brilliant time to be a communicator of truth. There's a genuine hunger for the real in an age of unreal. I regularly try to paint for preachers a picture of what it will be like in heaven one day. About a billion years from now, we'll have come back from riding around the far side **We'll be seated at yet another stunning banquet, marveling at an existence in which we never grow old.** of some galaxy on a heavenly white horse, having drunk our fill of eternal companionship with Jesus for yet another day.

We'll be seated at yet another stunning banquet, marveling at an existence in which we never grow old and never tire of joy unspeakable, and right in the midst of our reverie, Jesus will gently touch us on the shoulder, and will introduce us to someone whose face seems vaguely familiar. It will turn out that this man or woman once sat under our teaching, and their life was transformed because of something we said.

At that time will come the realisation that great teaching has an eternal payoff. Someone who was maybe headed for a Christless eternity, is now living forever, because we tried our very best to set forth God's truths in the most imaginative way we could muster. At that moment, every earthly trial, every great building, every grand endeavour will pale in the radiance of His smile, as he reminds us again, "Well done!"

This is our time! Make every presentation excellent! Remember the words of Charles Swindoll, who reminded me of a reality that has become something of a personal life – compass in recent years.

The sun didn't come up this morning for any reason other than the fact that God's not satisfied with the count yet.

Gather the harvest!

Notes

Chapter 1
Capturing the Imagination
1. Elmer Bendiner, The Fall of Fortresses

Chapter 2
The Pursuit of Excellence
1. George Hunter, Asbury Theological Seminary
2. Bill Hybels "Our Modern Moral Trifecta: Abortion"
   Willow Creek Community Church, March 14, 1993
3. John Ortberg, "It all goes back in the Box."
   Willow Creek community Church, December 1994

Chapter 3
Everyone has a Story
1. Steve Hartman, CBS News
2. "Reputations, Martin Luther King," BBC Documentary 1977

Chapter 6
We need heroes
1. Jon Meacham, Newsweek January 27, 1997

Chapter 7
We need Perspective
1. World Health Organisation, Geneva, 1998.

Chapter 8
Collecting Stories from Everywhere
1. Jeff Meyers, American Way Inflight Magazine 1998
2. Malcolm Linton, Time, September 13, 1999

Chapter 9
Staying current
1. Kate Belgrave "Does anybody still believe in forever?" New Zealand Herald
   [date unknown]

2. Rosemary McLeod, "Teenage abortion rate highlights generation Gap." Sunday Star-Times January 3, 1999.
3. John Ortberg: "The Attitude of Commitment" Willow Creek Community Church, August 3rd, 1997.
4. Kate Belgrave, New Zealand Herald, July 4th 2000
5. Kathryn Burnett, "Talking Dirty", Grace Magazine
6. Jill Jamieson ,"And when the trumpet sounds up yonder..." New Zealand Herald
7. Alan Duff "Sobering thoughts on turning 50." Christchurch Press, January 4th 2000.
8. Catherine Whitney "Seeking the Treads on Stairway to faith." USA Today June 3rd 1999

Chapter 11
Selecting Your Subjects
1. Kate Belgrave, "Deep Breath, ready for zero-zero." New Zealand Herald, August 25th, 1998
2. Rob Harley "Y2K – What me, worry?" Willow Creek Association of New Zealand Magazine, September 1999
Sources for this article included:
Revelation Series by John Ortberg, Willow Creek Community Church
Dave Hunt: "Y2K – a reasoned response to mass hysteria" Harvest House Publishers
Richard Abanes: "End Time Visions" Broadman and Holman Publishers
Newsweek [various articles]
New Zealand Herald [various]

Chapter 13
The Remarkable Ones
1. John Douglas, William Heinemann/Arrow "Mindhunter." pp 296-7. Reprinted by permission of the Random House Group Ltd.

Chapter 14
Retelling the Story
1. John Ortberg ,"The Attitude of Commitment" ibid
2. John Ortberg, "Overcoming Spiritual Procrastination" Willow Creek Community Church, June 2000

Chapter 17
Trends – Final Thoughts
1. Todd Gitlin "Pop Goes the Culture" U.S. News and World Report, June 1st, 1998
2. "Sin stakes new claim on NZ minds," New Zealand Herald, August 18th, 2001

About the Author

Rob Harley is a journalist, documentary-maker and former pastor. For more than 25 years he worked in television news and current affairs, for TVNZ – New Zealand's main television broadcaster. In his role as an investigative reporter and producer, Rob traveled extensively, covering assignments in places like Kosovo, Cambodia, East Timor and India. He's received more than twenty national and international awards for broadcasting, including two Gold Medals at the New York Film and Television Awards.

He currently specialises in teaching communication skills to both church and secular speakers, and lectures widely on contemporary Christian issues.

Rob is married to Alison, and they have two children, Ben and Kate.